MW00443767

GRANDMA GRACE'S
SOUTHERN FAVORITES

GRANDMA GRACE'S SOUTHERN FAVORITES

VERY, VERY OLD RECIPES ADAPTED FOR A NEW GENERATION

MARTY DAVIDSON

RUTLEDGE HILL PRESS
Nashville, Tennessee
A Division of Thomas Nelson Publishers
Since 1798

www.thomasnelson.com

Copyright © 2005 by Marty Davidson.

All rights reserved. No portion of this book may be reproduced, stored in a retrieval system, or transmitted in any form or by any means—electronic, mechanical, photocopy, recording, or any other—except for brief quotations in printed reviews, without prior permission of the publisher.

Published by Rutledge Hill Press, a Division of Thomas Nelson Publishers, P.O. Box 141000, Nashville, Tennessee 37214.

Rutledge Hill Press books may be purchased in bulk for educational, business, fundraising, or sales promotional use. For information, please e-mail SpecialMarkets@ThomasNelson.com.

This book is sold without any warranties of any kind, express or implied, and the publisher and author disclaim any liability for injury, loss, or damage caused by the contents of this book.

Illustrations of hearth and cookware (pages xiv, 30–33) by Alicia Adkerson.
Illustrations of food by Tonya Pitkin.

Library of Congress Cataloging-in-Publication Data

Davidson, Marty.
  Grandma Grace's southern favorites : very, very old recipes adapted for a new generation / Marty Davidson.
    p. cm.
  Includes index.
  ISBN 1-4016-0219-3 (hardcover)
  1. Cookery, American—Southern style. I. Title.
  TX715.2.S68D435 2005
  641.5975—dc22   2005008215

Printed in the United States of America
05 06 07 08 09 — 5 4 3 2 1

TO GRANDMA GRACE,
WHO MADE THIS BOOK POSSIBLE

Down where the sun's most always shining,
Where poverty clouds have a silver lining,
Where there's chicken and corn bread with every dining,
That's where the South begins.

Down where knighthood's still in flower,
Where they marry for love without a dower,
Where money is useful, but not a power,
That's where the South begins.

Down where the latch-string's outside the door,
Where a friend's a friend, whether rich or poor,
Where they trace their ancestry back to Noah,
That's where the South begins.

—Anonymous

CONTENTS

⫷ ACKNOWLEDGMENTS ⫸

I thank relatives and friends who were helpful in making these recipes usable. The excerpts from Grandma Grace's "receipt books for everyday living," which appear throughout the book, come from the following sources: *Dr. Chase's Recipes, or Information for Everybody: An Invaluable Collection of About Eight Hundred Practical Recipes* by A. W. Chase, M.D. (Ann Arbor: 1867); *Mackenzie's Five Thousand Receipts in All the Useful and Domestic Arts: Constituting a Complete Practical Library by an American Physician* (Pittsburgh: Troutman & Hayes, 1852); *The Housekeeper Cook Book* (Minneapolis: The Housekeeper Publishing Company, 1894); *Useful Knowledge, or A Familiar and Explanatory Account of the Various Productions of Nature, Mineral, Vegetable and Animal Which Are Chiefly Employed for the Use of Man* by Rev. William Bingley, A.M.F.L.S. (Philadelphia: A. Small, 1818).

GRANDMA GRACE'S SOUTHERN FAVORITES

⚊ INTRODUCTION ⚊

$\mathcal{I}$f you are looking for excellent cooking with a taste of the Old South, you will find it in these pages. Within each recipe, enhancing the taste, you'll discover a dreamy mixture of southern culture, down-home warmth, and family pride.

Chicken and Cloud-Tender Dumplin's, Gingersnap Gravy, Aunt Ella's Green Tomato Pie, Apple Cider Cake. These recipes have been passed down from generation to generation in my family, and I want to share them with a new generation that is hungry for wholesome southern cooking. When you fix these recipes and read the fascinating family stories accompanying them, you'll feel like you are basking in the flavors, tastes, smells, and warmth of the Old South. Enjoy!

HOW THIS BOOK CAME TO BE

I had been wondering what I could possibly do with the collection of outdated recipes Grandma Grace left me. I opened the shoebox of old cooking recipes, some penciled on scraps of paper, but most in narrow writing tablets with front covers wrinkled, corners missing. All were brown-spotted from age. Some headings indicated their origin—from Aunt Hezzie, Cousin Ludie Mae, even her mother, Rachel, who practiced her cooking expertise before and during the Civil War. They were enchanting, with their "pinch" of this, "dab" of that. Gazing at first one, then another, they somehow seemed familiar. Suddenly, I realized the recipes were for food I was brought up on, only they were written in "fireplace language."

In the old days, instructions in recipes (called "receipts" in the 1800s and earlier) were so skimpy and vague they appeared to be written only for the experienced cook. The usual directions were "take a few," "put in a handful of," "scatter a few pinches," and the like. Some of Grandma Grace's recipes had quaint instructions and terms not readily understandable, and some had no instructions at all.

Another part of my inheritance involved "receipts" that were not instructions for food but for everyday living. Grandma had saved "receipt" books published between 1818 and 1894 that offered advice on topics such as using milk to paint the barn, curing ulcers with carrots, and mending broken glass with garlic juice. I removed these books from the brown paper bags that Grandma had declared kept the bugs away. As I thumbed through the pages, I came across facts that Grandma had instilled deeply in me, reminding me of the tremendous influence she had on my life. She and Grandpa Ned lived within walking distance of our house, and I spent many days with her. During these visits, she described in great detail the old ways of life, explaining decades-old methods she still practiced. Later, I realized her stories included subtle messages about the best way to handle ordinary incidents in everyday life.

Both the cooking recipes and the receipts for everyday living were exceptional because they captured a way of life in the Old South that has now disappeared. Grandma wanted me to preserve them for our future kin, but some scraps and pages were already so disintegrated, they would be short-lived.

As I sat mulling over what to do with Grandma's treasures, dozens of images of my early childhood ran through my head. Suddenly, her big fireplace loomed before me. She was kneeling in front of the fire with the long bill of her bonnet pulled forward to protect her face, shiny with homemade cold cream. When I asked why she didn't use her little wood-burning cookstove that sat in the corner of the kitchen, she said she couldn't keep an even temperature in it like she could with fireplace coals. I already knew there was no equal to the scrumptious taste of her lemon meringue pie baked in the Dutch oven on red embers pulled a little forward onto the hearth.

I remembered Grandma laughing when she told me how hard it had been to get used to her new cookstove. She washed the turnip greens, put them in the black bucket-pot, and hung the pot over the fireplace as she had done in the past. All at once, she remembered she should have put the greens in her new aluminum boiler and set it on her new wood-burning cookstove.

Then came a vivid picture of Grandma removing the damp piece of brown paper bag from around the calf of my leg. She untied the string, rolled it up, carefully laid it aside for next time, and then looked for the purple bruise. It was gone. It had vanished. I was delighted that I could wear my frilly organdy Easter dress with pride. She loved that brown bag remedy to fade bruises.

While my mind traveled, I almost felt Grandma's thin, freckled hand saturating my sprained ankle with toad ointment she'd made by creaming toad frogs cooked tender in a boiler at the fireplace. I'd hurt my ankle when I stepped in a hole picking purple rooster violets in the woods behind her house. She kept the ointment in a pint fruit jar in the cellar sitting on the shelf in front of jars of canned peas, beans, and pickled peaches.

I blinked and there we were—Grandma and I were sitting in the sunken, hair-fringed, cowhide seats of the old rocking chairs on her wide front porch, gently moving them with our feet. She was smiling and telling about how she stole Grandpa Ned from his Yankee fiancée with a love potion she made of roots from the woods. Suddenly, her rocker stopped. Her head lowered. She stared at the floor. After a long pause and a big breath, she looked toward the sky and began telling about Grandpa kissing her behind a buggy during intermission at a barn dance. Before she realized it, she kissed him back. Ashamed, she had him take her straight home. That night, tears wet her pillow from the disgrace she'd brought on herself. She knew if he didn't marry her, she was ruined. She was already tainted from being seen with him, a carpetbagger. Everybody knew carpet-baggers were not accepted in the South. Regardless of the ridicule, she could not give him up. After they married, the community finally accepted him because of his gener-ous help in barn raisings and other community activities.

I loved that story. I had her tell it to me time after time.

After the enjoyment of reliving part of my younger life, I pulled my thoughts back to the present. I knew what I had to do—I had to come up with a plan to keep alive our her-itage from the Old South. For Grandma. And for myself. At that instant, I saw her smile.

I gathered the piles of bills and other papers on my desk and placed them in a drawer. With the desktop free, I set the shoebox of recipes beside the old books of infor-mation Grandma and Grandpa had lived by. My heart was light. I realized what a prize I had: the honest-to-goodness ways of ordinary folks in the Old South.

Thoughts whirled in my head like a monstrous cyclone. Maybe I could compile all the information in a book. A *book?* How could I write a book with Grandma's food recipes intertwined with material in her and Grandpa's beloved books for everyday living?

For days, I pondered how to dovetail both subjects under one cover. Then in bed one night, I awoke all excited and rose to a sitting position. There, propped on my elbows, I had the answer. I would start with Grandma's old Fireplace Recipes and add the current method that family members had revised over the years to accommodate available ingredients and cooking methods—recipes our family and relatives use today to produce the same fine taste and quality of the old fireplace cooking. This would be the Modern Method, recipes from which anyone could actually prepare down-home southern meals. To add even more flavor to each recipe, I would also include the special memories and family stories associated with each one.

And excerpts from the receipt books for everyday living—I would sprinkle these through-out the cookbook as sidebars. Combined with the food recipes and some background informa-tion on fireplace cooking, they would complete the picture of Grandma Grace's Old South.

And that is how this book came to be.

Beverages

⤜⤙ BISCUIT COFFEE ⤜⤙

*G*randpa loved his cup of coffee after supper, but real coffee often kept him awake for several hours. When Grandma substituted this hot drink, his taster didn't know the difference. He went to bed early and snored and snorted till she turned him on his side and chocked him with a pine cone–stuffed pillow. (She said.)

FIREPLACE RECIPE:

Take graham flour*, about half a gallon; cornmeal sifted half as much; fresh-churned butter 2 large lumps; molasses, pour to 4 pats of gentle foot[†]; sour milk and saleratus[‡] as for biscuit.

Bake in Dutch Oven over very slow coals 6 or 7 hours, or until browned through to color of coffee. One biscuit boiled in water an hour is plenty for 2 cups of coffee. Strain. Serve with cream and fine sugar as other coffee. A pinch of ground coffee before boiling adds to the taste.

MODERN METHOD:

Biscuits

2 cups whole wheat flour	1/4 cup dark cane molasses
1 cup cornmeal	1 1/2 cups sour milk or buttermilk[§]
3/4 teaspoon baking soda	2 tablespoons butter or margarine, melted

Preheat the oven to 375°. Combine the flour, cornmeal, and soda. Add the molasses, buttermilk, and melted butter. Mix lightly until combined, but do not overmix. Pour the mixture onto a floured surface, and knead the dough gently two or three times, handling the dough as little as possible. With floured hands, pat out the dough to about 1/2 inch thick. Using a floured cutter of desired size, cut out the biscuits. Place the biscuits on a greased sheet one inch apart. Bake for 15 to 18 minutes. Remove. Turn the oven down to 200°. Split the biscuits into halves, return to the oven, and let remain for 3 hours. Turn off the heat and leave

---

* Wheat coarsely ground, not sifted.
† Counting slowly to three between pats.
‡ Baking soda.
§ To make 1 cup sour milk, remove 1 tablespoon milk and replace it with 1 tablespoon lemon juice or vinegar.

in the oven another hour, or until the oven is cold or until the biscuits are browned through. *Makes 10 to 12 biscuits.*

To Make 1 Cup of Coffee

1   biscuit (see recipe above), cut in half   Milk or cream and sugar (optional)
1½ cups water   ¼ teaspoon butter
½ teaspoon ground coffee

Place the biscuit halves in a saucepan, add the water, bring to a boil, and then slow-simmer 45 minutes, or until 1 cup liquid remains. Add the ground coffee and boil 3 more minutes. Remove from the heat, whip, and strain through a cloth. Add the milk or cream and sugar as desired and serve hot, as coffee. Add the butter per cup. *Makes 1 cup of coffee.*

NOTE: The Fireplace Recipe yields more coffee than the Modern Method because in the old days biscuits were at least 3 inches in diameter; today's biscuits are about 2½ inches in diameter.

AGUE

Soot Coffee has cured many cases of ague*, after "everything else" had failed; it is made as follows:

Soot scraped from a chimney, (that from stove pipes does not do,) 1 table-spoon, steeped in water 1 pt., and settled with 1 egg beaten up in a little water, as for other coffee, with sugar and cream, 3 times daily with the meals, in place of other coffee.

It has come in very much to aid restoration in Typhoid Fever, bad cases of Jaundice, Dyspepsia, &c., &c.

—From *Dr. Chase's Recipes* (1867)

*Chills and fever.

ACORN COFFEE

*G*randma's Cherokee Indian friend and fourth cousin, Mahalia, advised her that Acorn Coffee cured many ailments of the heart, liver, and intestines and also removed nervous complaints. Acorns are bitter, but Grandma got around this by concocting this palatable recipe.

FIREPLACE RECIPE:

Take sound, ripe, big acorns, hull, then boil in water in hanging kettle a little time and throw bitter water out. Repeat a second time. A third time if needed. Spread acorns in the sun until completely dry. Parch in spider pan over slack coals, continually stir same, care not to burn, as they roast quicker than coffee. As acorns have no oil as coffee, add dollop of butter while hot. Cover and shake pan.

When cool, take of acorns, grind to a powder, grinding preferable to pounding. Mix 6 big spoons of powder with a third that of parched and ground coffee and 6 coffee cups of water for same number of drinkers. Boil a few minutes, strain through a bag of close cloth. Add a few grains of salt, sweeten with fine sugar to taste, with or without milk.

MODERN METHOD:

Ground Roasted Acorns

2   cups sound, ripe acorns, hulled
1   teaspoon butter or margarine, melted

Cover the acorns with water and boil 10 minutes. Discard the water. Repeat two times. Dry the acorns thoroughly in a 150° oven or at room temperature. Place in a low-sided pan in a 350° oven to roast. After 3 minutes, reduce the heat to 325°. Stir every 2 or 3 minutes until nicely browned, usually 15 to 20 minutes total, depending on the size of the acorns. Remove from the heat. Cover the acorns with the butter by stirring and shaking the pan. Cool the acorns, grind them in a coffee grinder, and place them in a tight container. *Makes 1 cup of Ground Roasted Acorns for 8 cups of coffee.*

To Make 1 Cup of Coffee

1   tablespoon Ground Roasted Acorns (see recipe above)
1   teaspoon regular ground coffee
    Few grains of salt
2   cups boiling water
    Milk or cream and sugar as desired

In a saucepan, place the Ground Roasted Acorns, coffee, salt, and boiling water. Simmer 5 minutes. Strain through a finely woven cloth, add milk or cream and sugar to taste, and drink hot as coffee. *Makes 1 cup of coffee.*

VARIATION: For *Dandelion Coffee*, make as above with 1 part roasted and ground dandelion root and 2 parts coffee.

HAIR RESTORATIVES AND INVIGORATORS (BALD HEADS)

Equal to Wood's, for a Trifling Cost.—Sugar of lead, borax, and lac-sulphur, of each 1 oz.; aqua ammonia ½ oz.; alcohol 1 gill. These articles to stand mixed for 14 hours; then add bay rum 1 gill; fine table salt 1 table-spoon; soft water 3 pts; essence of bergamot 1 oz.

This preparation not only gives a beautiful gloss, but will cause hair to grow upon bald heads arising from all common causes; and turn gray hair to a dark color.

Manner of Application.—When the hair is thin or bald, make two applications daily, until this amount is used up, unless the hair has come out sufficiently to satisfy you before that time; work it to the roots of the hair with a soft brush or the ends of the fingers, rubbing well each time.

For gray hair one application daily is sufficient. It is harmless and will do all that is claimed for it, does not cost only a trifle in comparison to the advertised restoratives of the day; and will be found as good or better than most of them.

—From *Dr. Chase's Recipes* (1867)

ᴄᴏ COFFEE IN THE POCKET ᴏᴄ

*G*randma kept a supply of this concentrated coffee on hand
to keep from having to parch and grind coffee too often.

FIREPLACE RECIPE:

Put some ground coffee in pan with about 3 times amount of water and boil down
to amount of coffee began with. A teaspoon or two in boiling water makes a good cup
of coffee.

MODERN METHOD:

Coffee Mix

2   cups ground coffee

6   cups water

Add the coffee to the water and boil down to 2 cups liquid. Cool, bottle in sterile canning
jars, and seal. *Makes 2 cups liquid, for 32 cups coffee.*

To Make 1 Cup of Coffee

1   tablespoon Coffee Mix (see recipe above)

1   cup boiling water

Add the Coffee Mix to the boiling water. Makes fine drinking. *Makes 1 cup of coffee.*

DISINFECTANT, FOR ROOMS

Coffee, dried and pulverized, then a little of it sprinkled upon
a hot shovel, will, in a very few minutes, clear a room of all
impure effluvia, and especially of an animal character.

—From *Dr. Chase's Recipes* (1867)

❧ FIREPLACE KITCHENS ❧

*T*he typical kitchen was large. Most were in a separate building connected to the main part of the house by a short breezeway-type covered walkway at floor level. The division was designed to prevent cooking odors from permeating the parlor and sleeping area and to keep those areas as cool as possible in summertime, while still allowing the family to cook a big meal. In winter the huge fireplace kept the kitchen warm and provided a cozy gathering place for the family.

Fires burned in the fireplace year-round since it took several hours for a fresh fire to burn down to proper cooking coals. At night ashes were banked on the unburned wood and hot coals. The next morning the ashes were raked away, wood was piled on them, and with the help of bellows or a cardboard fan, in no time the fire was burning as if it had never died down.

Ingredients for cooking that were not readily available from the garden or woods were obtained from vendors called "drummers." Most housekeepers preferred to get supplies from a traveling drummer who made regular trips through the region and who carried a variety of needed items. From him, they learned all the hush-hush news in the area.

Fireplace cooking was a natural for most young girls. Drilled into them was the noteworthy proverb written by Owen Meredith (1831–1891):

We may live without poetry, music and art;
We may live without conscience, and live without heart;
We may live without friends; we may live without books;
But civilized man can not live without cooks.

Girls learned to prepare superb meals by helping their mothers and grandmothers in the kitchen. Since entertainment was self-made, they found excitement in combining ingredients to make a tasty dish. An old axiom says that almost any woman can cook well if she has plenty of ingredients, but the real science of cooking is to be able to create a good dish or meal with very little.

∽ COW-LESS MILK ∽

*G*randma loved to tell about learning to make this milk. After the Civil War, carpetbaggers settled in the area of Georgia where she lived. They had no belongings except what they stuffed into a carpetbag, but somehow improvised to fill their needs. When Grandpa caught one "borrowing" peanuts from his field, he called it square with the carpetbagger in exchange for this recipe for Cow-less Milk.

FIREPLACE RECIPE:

Take a double handful of raw peanuts, shelled, and put through grinder two or three times until fine as can get. Put to this twice as much fresh spring water and whip. Should be thin. Combine a little honey, a vanilla bean with same and heat lightly but do not boil.

While hot, strain out lumps and husks and let stand until cold before using. Nice drink especially for children.

Make different flavors with different nuts.

MODERN METHOD:

1 cup raw peanuts finely ground	1 tablespoon honey
2 cups water	1/4 teaspoon vanilla

Combine the peanuts, water, honey, and vanilla in a blender or mix by hand until smooth. Remove the mixture, place it in a saucepan, and warm to 100°. Do not boil. Strain through fine cheesecloth.

Should have a delicate flavor. If more water is desired, to each 1/4 cup of added water, add 1/4 teaspoon honey. Serve cold. *Makes 2 cups.*

VARIATIONS: For different flavors, use pecans, cashews, Brazil nuts, or other nuts.

❧ MILK-ADE ❧

*G*randma said when she was a child, her mother made this for the children to drink while the grown-ups had their four o'clock coffee.

FIREPLACE RECIPE:

Take some rich milk and as much boiling water. Put in some orange rind and a little juice. Cook to a boil then add sugar to taste. Strain if desired.

MODERN METHOD:

1	cup milk	1	cup boiling water
4	tablespoons sugar		
2	tablespoons orange juice		
	Grated rind of 1 medium-size orange		

In a saucepan, bring the milk to a full boil over high heat. Remove from the stove immediately. Place the sugar, orange juice, and orange peel in a heatproof pitcher and add the boiling water. Cool and combine with the milk. When cold, strain the mixture. Serve hot or cold. *Makes 2¼ cups.*

MILK PAINT, FOR BARNS—ANY COLOR

"Mix water lime with skim-milk, to a proper consistence to apply with a brush, and it is ready to use. It will adhere well to wood, whether smooth or rough, to brick, mortar or stone, where oil has not been used, (in which case it cleaves to some extent,) and forms a very hard substance, as durable as the best oil paint. It is too cheap to estimate, and any one can put it on who can use a brush." —Country Gentleman.

—From *Dr. Chase's Recipes* (1867)

❧ PEAHULL BEER ❧

*W*hen Uncle Henry had a hankering to make Peahull Beer, Aunt Hezzie shelled a bushel of peas at a time to get his hulls. Then, along with the family, he had to suffer through eating peas for breakfast, dinner, and supper until he began covering them with Pepper Catsup (see page 129). Then he hollered for more peas—and catsup.

FIREPLACE RECIPE:

Fill a boiler with green hulls of field or Crowder peas, pour on water till it rises a quarter of a finger above the shells, put in a little ginger root, bruised, very little sugar, if any, and simmer over slow fire for 3 hours. Strain off the liquor, and add a strong decoction of wood sage, or the hop, so as to render it pleasantly bitter, then ferment in the usual manner. A fortnight should do it. Cook peas separately.

MODERN METHOD:

2 cups young sage leaves finely chopped and packed
2 gallons green pea shells, field or Crowder
1/2 teaspoon ground ginger
   Sugar if desired

Place the sage leaves in a large pot, pour green pea shells on top, and add water until it rises a half-inch above the shells. Sprinkle in the ginger and mix. Cover and simmer over a low fire for 3 hours. Taste. Add the sugar if desired.

Remove from the heat, strain through a coarse cloth into a noncorrosive container, and press the pulp in the cloth as dry as possible to gain all the strength. Discard the pulp. Leave the liquid open to ferment for 14 days. Skim. *Makes 2 (6-ounce) bottles.*

✃ GINGER BEER ✃

*C*ousin Lizzie kept a supply of this beer put away for Uncle Jeb to drink before she used her bee-sting treatment on him for his arthritis. After a few mugsful, he never knew when she held a raging bee to his knee to shoot in its venomous stinger.

FIREPLACE RECIPE:

Take 18 gallons of good spring water and with it boil most of 20 pounds of sugar and 1 pound of honey and take from fire. Bruise a pound of good Jamaica ginger and add this and remaining sugar to the hot liquid.

Grind 5 or 6 pounds raisins and add to the whole with the juice and peel of a dozen middling sized lemons. When the liquid is blood warm, put in a quarter-pint of good solid ale yeast. Pour all in open crock and let stand a fortnight. Skim as necessary.

Put a thick layer of straw at bottom to filter it.

MODERN METHOD:

1	gallon water less $^1/_2$ cup to use later	1	ounce gingerroot finely chopped
1	plus 1 cups sugar	1	package active dry yeast
$^1/_2$	cup honey	1	cup raisins, chopped
$^1/_4$	teaspoon ground ginger	1	unpeeled lemon, sliced

In a large pot, place the water, except $^1/_2$ cup to use later. Add 1 cup of the sugar and the honey. Boil 5 minutes and remove from the heat. Mix the remaining 1 cup sugar with the ginger and gingerroot, and add to the hot liquid. Warm the saved $^1/_2$ cup water and mix with the yeast.

Stir the raisins and lemon slices into the hot mix, and when cool, add the yeast mixed with the warm water. Pour the mixture into a noncorrosive container, cover with coarse cheesecloth, and let stand in a warm room to ferment at least 3 weeks or until bubbles cease. Skim as needed. Strain through muslin cloth and bottle; seal with cork stoppers. *Makes 1 gallon.*

⤜ APPLE BEER ⤛

*A*t church, a fellow was shot in the forehead by young boys with a peashooter. Before he yelled for help, he took out his bottle of Apple Beer and took a big swig.

FIREPLACE RECIPE:

Take 12 to 15 apples and peel. Put peelings in sun or spread on hearth to dry a good day or so. Rasp the apples peeled and cored across the grater and place in a stone crock. To this add dry peelings and a short 3 gallons good fresh spring water.

Stir the whole every day for a week then put to it 4 or 5 pints white sugar or sweet as wanted, and season with several spoons of ginger root, bruised well, a stick or two of cinnamon and a few cloves, all as liked.

Let stay till the morrow, strain through muslin and bottle. After a week it is ready.

MODERN METHOD:

8 apples, any kind, about 2^1/$_2$ pounds	1^1/$_3$ ounces gingerroot, bruised
1^1/$_3$ gallons water	^{1}/$_4$ teaspoon ground cloves
3 cups white sugar	^{1}/$_2$ teaspoon cinnamon
1 cup brown sugar	

Peel and core the apples. Separate the peelings and place in the sun or warm place for a day or two until thoroughly dry. The peelings contain the yeast to ferment.

Grate the apples into a noncorrosive container. Add the water and peelings. Let season 7 days, stirring every day. Strain.

Add the sugars, gingerroot, cloves, and cinnamon and let stand overnight. Strain through a cloth and bottle. Let stand another 7 days to mellow before using. *Makes about 6 quarts.*

◌ MUSCADINE (GRAPE) WINE ◌

*W*ith a few exceptions, nothing was wasted at Grandma's. After making Muscadine Wine for a wedding reception, she set the hulls aside to boil and can. Weeks later she found them and poured them in the hog trough, unknown to Grandpa. After the hogs lay in the pen in a dazed condition a day and a half, Grandpa went for the veterinarian. He came and made the hogs well by poking them with a stick. His fee was nominal.

FIREPLACE RECIPE:

Use firm muscadines, wash good, and mash. To every gallon of muscadines pour 1 quart boiling water and let stand a full day. Then strain through a cloth and mash out juice. To every gallon of juice, put in 2 or 3 pounds best white sugar. Let stand another day or two.

Strain into bottles and cover tops with cloth. Save out a little juice which ever so often pour into bottles to overflow and rid of scum. Let stand 2 or 3 months or more. Strain again through a cloth bag. Bottle and cork and let stand another month or so before using.

MODERN METHOD:

4   quarts muscadine grapes, scuppernong or Concord
1   quart boiling water
1¼ cups sugar to every quart of juice

Wash the grapes. Place them in a 1½-gallon noncorrosive container, break open the hulls with a potato masher, and add boiling water. Let stand 24 hours, then strain through a cloth and press out as much juice as possible. Discard the strainings. To every quart of juice, add 1¼ cups sugar. Mix well. Let stand another 24 hours.

Strain the juice into bottles and cover the tops with medium-thickness cloth. Save out a little juice and once a week for 3 weeks, pour some into the bottles to flow out the scum that has risen.

Let stand 2 or 3 months more. Strain again, then bottle and cork and let stand at least a month before using. *Makes about 2 quarts.*

↬ BLACKBERRY WINE ↫

*W*hen Grandpa made a keg of Blackberry Wine, Grandma took the seeds pressed from the berries and scattered them in the woods to replenish the old vines. A few years later there was a bramble fence it took all the men in the community to tear away.

FIREPLACE RECIPE:

Use ripe berries or the wine will be harsh and hard. If fruit is too ripe, the wine will be faint, low, and bland.

Clean, mash thoroughly one gallon ripe berries and barely cover same with water. Let stand several days to ferment. Strain. To juice, add ¼ as much fine white sugar. Save out a little juice and pour the balance in bottles or jugs, filling to the brim, in order that as the juice ferments, the scum will flow off. For a week or 10 days following, pour juice into bottle to flow off all scum. Close jugs lightly.

After a week, cork tight and let stand in a cool place for a few months before using.

MODERN METHOD:

1   gallon ripe blackberries, cleaned and mashed
    Sugar (berries vary in content of juice; use 1 pint sugar to 4 pints juice, or to taste)

Wash and crush the berries. Place in a large noncorrosive pan or crock. Add water to cover and let stand 3 days. Strain through medium-weave cloth, pressing to obtain as much juice as possible. Discard the mash. Reserve half a cup of juice, and to the balance add the sugar and stir until well dissolved. Strain and bottle in 5 (10-ounce) bottles.

Each day for 7 days, pour a little of the reserved juice into the bottles to flow off the scum that has not bubbled out. Close the bottles very lightly.

After another 7 days, if no scum has arisen, cork tightly and let stand in a cool place for 3 to 5 months before using. Makes a fine wine. *Makes 5 (10-ounce) bottles.*

❧ WHEY WINE ❧

*G*randma said this was originally concocted to soothe sore throats, but with a little added wine (plus a jig), it turned into Grandpa's toddy.

FIREPLACE RECIPE:

Save a little whey from clabber before putting into churn. Add a little fresh milk and same of favorite wine. Boil and strain.

MODERN METHOD:

2   cups milk   1   cup favorite wine

Boil the milk. Add the wine and remove from the heat at the first bubble. Let stand until the curd is separated from the whey, and then strain the mixture through a porous cloth. Serve as is, iced or heated. A good drink anytime, but especially for those in poor health. *Makes 4 cups.*

CATARRH, OR COLD

Symptoms:—A dull pain in the head, swelling and redness of the eyes, the effusion of thin acrid mucus from the nose, hoarseness, fever, cough, &c.

Treatment:—If the symptoms be violent, bleed and give twenty drops of hartshorn in a half pint of warm vinegar whey. Hoarhound and boneset tea, taken in large quantities, are very useful.

The patient should be confined to his bed, and be freely purged. If there is great pain in the breast, apply a blister to it. To ease cough, take 2 tea-spoons-ful of No. 1 every 15 minutes, or till relief is obtained.

The influenza is nothing more than an aggravated state of catarrh, and is to be cured by the same remedies. No cough or cold is too light to merit atten-tion. Neglected colds lay the foundation of diseases that every year send thou-sands to the grave.

No. 1. Cough mixture. Paregoric, half an ounce, syrup of squills,* 1 oz., antimonial wine, 2 drachms, water, six ounces. Dose is 2 teaspoonfuls every fifteen minutes till the cough abates.

*Sea onion.   —From *Mackenzie's Five Thousand Receipts* (1852)

⊂⊃ MINT JULEP ⊂⊃

Grandpa used to brag that Grandma had her own secret receipt to make the best Mint Julep in the whole state of Dixie. She finally let out the secret: mint juice. She admitted that sometimes she barely had enough leaves for one tankard of julep. This was when she forgot to put a dash of snuff in the holes before she planted the mint, and cutworms enjoyed most of the leaves—leaving the plants straggly as a molting hen. With snuff, our tasters couldn't tell the difference, but the worms' tasters seemed to.

She never dared waste any extra mint leaves, so she boiled and cooled them and patted the water on her face to tighten her wrinkles.

FIREPLACE RECIPE:

Take a little handful of peppermint leaves and chop them right fine to a tablespoon and put them in a silver tankard. Take back of the spoon and mash the mint against the side until the leaves are mushy and shiny. Pulping the leaves fine-tunes the taste.

Add a piling-up teaspoon regular sugar and just enough water to dissolve it and whirl with the spoon to mix in the leaves. And set it away in a cool place for at least an hour.

Pour in a quarter cup of Papa's favorite mellow Kentucky bourbon and jiggle the arm to add a little more, then pour it into the tankard which fill with finely cracked ice. Top it with a lively sprig of damp mint dipped in fine powdered sugar to coat and let it set a few minutes. Then it is ready for a king. Make only one tankard at a time.

MODERN METHOD:

The same basic recipe is used today.

Breads and Cereals

☙ SPATTER BREAD ❧

*I*n the sharecropper's shanty where Grandma and Grandpa lived while they built their house, Grandma rose up from the fireplace holding a skillet of bread and looked into the beady eyes of a blacksnake. His head was a few inches into the room, emerging near the mantle where broken chimney mortar had left a hole. When she threw her hands up in fright, the skillet fell to the floor, overturning, and batter spattered everywhere. The snake never knew it was Grandma's hoe handle that mushed him in the mortar between the bricks on the outside chimney wall. From then on, this was "Spatter Bread."

FIREPLACE RECIPE:

Sift together a pint of fresh-ground white cornmeal, 2 or 3 heavy dashes of salt, and a big kitchen spoon of baking powder. Put to this several eggs beat to a froth, then a little melted butter, fresh churned, a short pint of fresh creamy milk, and a half pint of cold boiled rice, and mix well the whole together. Sprinkle a handful of dry cornmeal on the sides and bottom of greased spider pan, cover, set same on trivet over a mound of hot coals, and bake. Have plenty butter on the table.

MODERN METHOD:

2	cups plus $^1/_4$ cup white cornmeal	3	tablespoons butter or margarine, melted
1	teaspoon salt	$1^1/_2$	cups milk
$1^1/_2$	teaspoons baking powder	1	cup cold boiled rice
3	eggs, well beaten		

Preheat the oven to 450°. Sift together the 2 cups cornmeal, salt, and baking powder. Add the eggs, then melted butter, milk, and rice. Blend thoroughly. Grease a 10-inch black iron skillet or heavy baking pan. Sprinkle the remaining $^1/_4$ cup dry cornmeal on the sides and bottom of the pan for extra crunch and easy removal of the bread. Spoon the mix into the skillet and bake 20 to 25 minutes until brown and the bread shrinks from sides of the pan. Serve hot with butter. *Makes 8 servings.*

❧ GRANDMA'S SKILLET ❧ CORN BREAD

Birds loved to eat the tender green sprouts of roasting-ear corn just as they sprouted out of the ground in Grandma's garden. She sat and shooed them away for a time, then smartened herself up. With a discarded, punctured inner tube from a tire on the Model T, she cut narrow strips and placed them in a wiggly fashion like snakes beside the rows of corn. She sat and laughed as the birds flew down, then swooped to the sky in lightning haste.

FIREPLACE RECIPE:

Place short quart of fresh whole milk in a pan over low fire and when very hot, put in 5 or 6 kitchen spoons of good bolted cornmeal, stirring milk before it hits. Keep stirring to a bubble, not to lump, and take up. To this add the proper saleratus*, salt, 2 or 3 big spoons hickory bacon drippings, and an egg size chunk of fresh churned butter. When cool, add two fresh laid eggs beat to one color.

Cook in spider on trivet until done. Spoon out. Take to the table with plenty butter.

MODERN METHOD:

6	slices hickory-smoked bacon	2	tablespoons butter, melted
3	cups milk	2	eggs, well beaten
1	cup cornmeal	2	teaspoons baking powder
3/4	teaspoon salt		

Fry the bacon in a black iron skillet or heavy frying pan. Remove when crisp, and discard the grease except for 2 teaspoons. Save the bacon for other purposes.

Preheat the oven to 350°. Place the milk in a saucepan over medium heat. When hot, add the cornmeal rapidly and stir briskly for 3 or 4 minutes. Remove from the heat. Add the salt, butter, and the 2 teaspoons of bacon drippings. Cool. Add the beaten eggs and baking powder. Use the skillet in which the bacon was fried, greasing the sides as well as the bottom. Pour the batter into the skillet. Batter should be about 1 inch thick. Bake in the preheated oven 25 to 30 minutes or until brown. Serve hot. Dish up with a spoon. *Makes 8 servings.*

*Baking soda.

❧ AUNT GUSSIE'S ROASTING- ❧
EAR SPOON BREAD

*W*hen Grandma was young, "bundling" was a ritual that more or less announced a couple was engaged. The couple slept in the same bed while fully clothed and if marriage didn't ensue, they were outcasts from society. The night Grandma bundled with Grandpa, she lay in bed on her side of the board that was placed upright down the middle of the bed. She had chosen the board instead of having her legs tied together. Waiting for Grandpa to get his lengthy talk from her pa, she thought of all the goodies she'd cook for him later, like Gussie's spoon bread.

FIREPLACE RECIPE:

Cut and scrape corn from a bunch of young roasting ears. Put to this several hefty spoons of cornmeal, a spoon or 2 of fine-grade sugar, 3 or so fresh-laid eggs and proper salt. Mix with a pint of warm sweet milk and a few dollops of fresh-churned butter, melted. Pour in pan and set in Dutch oven with 2 fingers of water.

Bake until done and tittle* with butter.

MODERN METHOD:

2½ cups milk	1 teaspoon sugar
1¾ cups fresh corn cut	1 teaspoon salt
coarsely from cob	3 egg yolks, well beaten
½ cup cornmeal	3 egg whites, stiffly beaten

¼ cup butter or margarine, melted, plus extra for topping

Preheat the oven to 300°. In a saucepan, heat the milk to room temperature. Stir in the corn and cornmeal and slowly simmer 8 to 10 minutes, stirring constantly. Add the ¼ cup butter, sugar, and salt. In a separate bowl or cup, spoon a little of the hot mixture into the well-beaten egg yolks while stirring briskly, and then add them to the hot mixture slowly while stirring. Remove from the heat. When slightly cool, fold the mixture into the beaten egg whites.

Pour into a buttered 2-quart casserole and bake for 45 minutes to 1 hour, or until the mix quivers only slightly in the center when shaken. Top with small pools of the additional melted butter. *Makes 8 servings.*

*A small amount, the size of the dot over the letter *i*.

❧ FATBACK SPOON BREAD ❧

*G*randma usually made this spoon bread when she boiled collard greens. Grandpa loved to alternate bites of spoon bread with the greens after he almost drowned them with sorghum syrup.

FIREPLACE RECIPE:

Take a half pound of fatback and wash off all possible salt, slice the same thin and fry brittle. Drain, but save a little of the bottom grease with meat particles. Set aside.

In a stew pan, put a half-pint of cornmeal and a handful of flour with a pint of good fresh sweet milk. Place over fire and stir until it is of a good thickness. Now add more milk, a half-pint, the bottom grease, proper baking powder, stir good, and taste for salt and add if needed.

Put in 4 eggs as thus: beat in the yolks, then add frothed whites gently. Crumble tender fatback into the whole and bake gently about an hour.

MODERN METHOD:

½	pound bacon	2	teaspoons baking powder
1	cup cornmeal	½	teaspoon salt, as desired
⅓	cup all-purpose flour	4	egg yolks, beaten creamy
2	plus 1 cups milk	4	egg whites

Preheat the oven to 350°. Cook the bacon until crisp, remove from the pan, and place on a paper towel to drain. Save 1 tablespoon of the drippings.

Place the cornmeal and flour in a saucepan, and gradually add 2 cups of the milk while beating the mix until smooth. Cook over low heat until thickened, stirring steadily. Add the remaining cup of milk, bacon drippings, baking powder, salt, and beaten egg yolks. Beat the egg whites to stiff peaks and fold them into the mixture. Last, crumble the bacon and blend in well. Bake in a 2-quart casserole about an hour or until a knife inserted in the center comes out clean. *Makes 8 servings.*

⤳ DIXIE CRACKLING BREAD ⤳

*G*randma often had a hankering for crackling bread when she was out of cracklings. The batch made from leftover skins in the lard-rendering process after killing hogs went so fast, occasionally she made a few cracklings for crackling bread by frying crisp the rind from the slab bacon.

FIREPLACE RECIPE:

Cut fatback with skin till a quart is filled with thumb size pieces. Cover with lard and cook in Dutch oven over hot coals till meat separates from skins. Pour away every iota of grease. Leave skins in oven and parch slow, stirring, take up when a little swollen.

Take a pint of cracklings, mash smaller, cover with hot water and let soak. Sift husk from quart of cornmeal, put dash of salt, pinch of soda. Put to this a pint of buttermilk, a little of the crackling grease from bottom, and stir smooth. Drain cracklings and add to the whole. Mix all well together to make a rather dry dough and shape into two pones. Put in covered Dutch oven having a little meat drippings and bake over medium quick coals like other bread till brown.

MODERN METHOD:

For cracklings, cut the rind from 1½ pounds of bacon and boil the rind in water until soft. Save the bacon for other purposes. Cut the boiled rind into 1-inch squares and cover with oil. Fry over high heat about 5 minutes, drain the oil from the pan, and cook the rinds in a dry pan over very low heat another 5 minutes, stirring constantly. Remove and drain. If not crisp when cold, refry without the fat. Due to differences in meat, frying time varies.

1	cup cracklings	2	cups cornmeal
½	teaspoon salt	1	cup buttermilk
½	teaspoon baking soda	1	tablespoon oil for frying

Preheat the oven to 425°. Break the cracklings into pieces, put in a bowl, and pour hot water to cover the cracklings. Let soak 3 or 4 minutes and then drain. Mix the salt and soda with the cornmeal; add the buttermilk and mix well. Stir in the cracklings. Make a dough stiff enough to handle.

Shape the dough into a pone (similar to French bread) not over 2½ inches high in the center, and place on a greased cookie sheet. Place in the hot oven. When the dough is slightly browned on top, reduce the heat to 350° and bake 30 to 40 minutes. Serve hot. *Makes 1 loaf for 6 servings.*

NOTE: Slice leftover crackling bread and fry in hot fat until brown for a delicious crisp treat.

⌒ BISCUIT SIZZLES ⌒

*A*unt Lillie served this creation with her roast beef and tasty dark brown gravy at the blowout celebrating her son's return from World War I.

FIREPLACE RECIPE:

Make a batch of rich biscuit dough and after kneading, pinch off pecan-size bits, let floured palms roll it into balls then give it a knuckle pat. Drop in hot lard and brown lightly on both sides. Roll in fine sugar specked with cinnamon while hot.

MODERN METHOD:

2 cups all-purpose flour	Kneading flour
2 teaspoons baking powder	Oil for frying
1 teaspoon salt	1 tablespoon sugar for sprinkling
1/2 cup plus 1 tablespoon milk	1/4 teaspoon cinnamon for sprinkling
1/4 cup cooking oil	

Sift the flour, baking powder, and salt into a mixing bowl. Combine the milk and oil, and add to the dry ingredients all at once. Stir until the dough clings together. Knead lightly on a floured board ten times. Roll out to 1/2-inch thickness and cut with a 2-inch biscuit cutter.

Drop the biscuits one or two at a time into sizzling hot oil. Fry about 1 minute on each side until evenly browned. Take out and drain on a paper towel.

Mix the sugar and cinnamon, and sprinkle the tops while hot. Or use the biscuits plain as croutons. Serve hot. *Makes 10 biscuits.*

FRIED BISCUITS WITH BEER GRAVY

*G*randma made this for special company, excluding the preacher.

FIREPLACE RECIPE:

Gravy. Make first. Mix together a short pint of medium or dark beer with a quarter pint of strong beef stock and a dollop of butter. To this put handful diced carrots, same of fine cut onions, then a faggot* of 8 or 10 stems bushy parsley, 1 of thyme, few sprigs celery leaves, bay leaf, tie with white thread, then a whole clove or two and salt. Boil all to tender, strain and put through fine sieve for pulp, add to juice. With pan over fire, thicken with a little flour. Serve hot with fried biscuits.

Biscuits. Make usual batch of dough, add more milk to batter. Drop hefty spoonfuls on hot griddle not to crowd. Brown both sides. Take up, brush tops with butter. Keep dry and crisp till all is ready.

MODERN METHOD:

Beer Gravy

1½ cups Apple Beer (see page 16) or other favorite (dark is best)

1 cup canned beef broth boiled down from 1½ cups

1¼ cups carrots, cut in small pieces

1¼ cups onions, finely chopped

1 faggot* of 10 stems parsley, 1 sprig celery leaves, 1 bay leaf

2 whole cloves

1½ tablespoons flour sifted with ½ teaspoon salt

1 tablespoon butter or margarine

Make the gravy first. Mix the beer, broth, carrots, onions, faggot, and cloves. Boil all together until the vegetables are tender. Remove from the heat. Discard the faggot and cloves. Strain and save the liquid. Purée the strained vegetables and add back to the liquid. Blend in the flour and simmer 3 to 4 minutes over low heat until slightly thickened. Beat until smooth. Stir in the butter. *Makes 3 cups.*

*A bundle tied together with thread or string.

Fried Biscuits

1	cup flour	1	tablespoon butter or margarine
2	teaspoons baking powder	1	tablespoon shortening
1/2	teaspoon sugar	3/4	cup milk (for thin batter)
1/4	teaspoon salt		

In a large mixing bowl, sift together the flour, baking powder, sugar, and salt. In a separate small bowl, mix the butter and shortening thoroughly with a fork. Blend the butter mixture into the flour mixture. Add the milk and beat the batter until smooth.

Drop separate tablespoons of the batter onto a medium-hot griddle to make a thin biscuit. Cook 4 to 5 minutes until done and browned, turning each once. Crisscross several table knives on a plate, take up the biscuits, and lay them over the knives to keep the bottoms dry while cooking the balance. Lightly brush the tops with butter or margarine. Reheat the gravy and serve all hot. *Makes 8 servings.*

ALCOHOL

For those who take any kind of spirits for the *sake* of the spirit, let me give you the following:

"SPIRITUAL FACTS.—That *whis-key* is the *key* by which many gain entrance into our prisons and almshouses.

That *brandy* brands the noses of all those who cannot govern their appetites.

That *punch* is the cause of many unfriendly *punches*.

That *ale* causes many ailings, while *beer* brings to the *bier*.

That *wine* causes many to take a *winding* way home.

That *cham-pagne* is the source of many *real* pains.

That *gin* slings that "slewed" more than *slings of olk*."

—From *Dr. Chase's Recipes* (1867)

❧ FIREPLACE UTENSILS ❧

*B*asic pots for open-hearth cooking were the Dutch oven, spider pan, and the kettle, or cauldron, all made of cast iron. Most had three legs, three or more inches long, allowing them to sit above or balance easily in the fire coals, which were usually from oak or hickory wood.

Dutch Oven

The medium-size Dutch oven, also known as the bake kettle, was basic, but it was helpful to have additional sizes. The Dutch oven had a long handle, three legs a few inches long, and a slightly convex lid with a one-inch lip around the edge to hold hot coals. With the Dutch oven sitting under a pile of coals on the hearth, heat was maintained evenly by adding or removing coals.

The Dutch oven was used for baking bread and other food and for roasting. For baking, it was always preheated in hot coals, and the lid was propped on the side of the pot to heat at the same time. Long-handled, iron pot hooks were used to move the pots and lids.

For cake baking, batter was usually poured into smaller pans called patty-pans and set in the Dutch oven. This prevented overdone bottoms. I am told my great-grandma lined the Dutch oven with layers of parchment paper to keep from burning the baked goods poured directly into the oven.

Dutch Oven

The Dutch oven was also used as a double boiler for sauces, custards, pie fillings, and other delicacies. With a small amount of water in the bottom of one pot, another pot containing the ingredients was set in the water and stirred with a long-handle spoon, the equivalent of the modern double-boiler.

Spider Pan

The spider pan was used mostly for frying. It was much like the Dutch oven except it was much more shallow. Quite versatile, it was used for frying meats and potatoes, sautéing, and some baking. It was easier to remove thin breads, cookies, and such from the spider pan than from the deep Dutch oven. The spider was usually set on very hot coals pulled out onto the hearth, which extended two feet or more into the room.

Spider Pan

Boiling Kettle

The boiling kettle was a deep pot. It had legs so it could be set in coals, but it was usually hung on large, iron, S-shaped hooks by its handle from a horizontal rod installed two and a half to three feet above the fireplace floor. These rods were above the center of the flame. More sophisticated fireplaces had a swinging crane secured by a vertical bar hinged to the side of the fireplace wall. The crane could be swung in and out so that the contents of the pot could be stirred away from the heat. Several kettles could be suspended from the crane over the fire by the S-hooks; the temperature of each kettle was controlled by its position on the crane and the number of hooks used. On both the rod and crane, S-hooks were used to lower or raise the kettle over the fire.

The kettle was used for boiling chunks of meat such as beef, venison, and whole fowl, and it was almost always used for cooking vegetables. While large amounts of greens boiled in the bottom of the pot, smaller pans of okra, carrots, or squash were stacked on the greens and cooked separately during one boiling. Nowadays that is called steaming.

Boiling Kettle

Saucepan

The saucepan was used for warming and for cooking small amounts of food such as sauces, gravies, and puddings. There were usually several sizes—1-quart, 2-quart, and 3-quart. Some had long legs so they could sit directly in a bed of coals and cook food that required very hot heat, and others had short legs for when less heat was desired.

Saucepan

Griddle Pan

A griddle with a flat bottom was used for cooking thin-batter cakes or pancakes called flapjacks. It was set on a trivet (see below) in coals on the hearth, unless there was a swinging arm holding a hanging shelf (see below) that could be raised and lowered with S-hooks. The arm was pulled forward from the heat, and the food turned to cook on the other side.

Hanging Shelf

The hanging shelf was very convenient for cooking directly over the fire.

Trivet

Trivets had legs of different lengths, some as long as eight inches. This allowed them to sit in thick beds of coals for very hot cooking.

Water Kettle

The smooth-bottomed, thick iron kettle for hot water usually sat on a shelf built into the side of the fireplace. There the water stayed hot. On fireplaces having no shelf, the kettle was placed in a nest of coals, and when boiling water was desired, it was set in a pile of very hot embers.

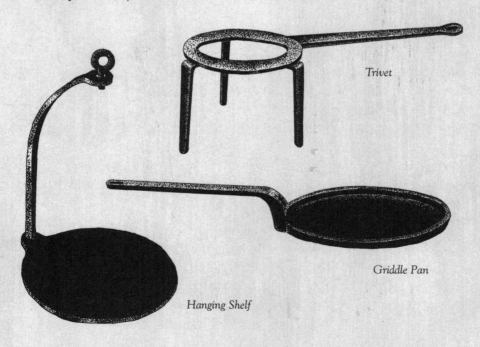

Trivet

Griddle Pan

Hanging Shelf

Coffee Grinder

Green coffee was roasted in the Dutch oven over a slow fire, constantly stirred until it browned, and then cooled and placed in an airtight container. It was always ground fresh in the coffee grinder as needed.

Coffee Pot

The coffee pot was a smooth-bottomed, heavily enameled cylindrical container just short of a foot tall. After boiling water was poured through ground coffee in a cloth sack that rested over the top, the pot was set on a trivet in hot coals and then removed. After the grounds were discarded, an egg was broken into the pot of coffee to collect the sediment. Most times a pinch of salt was added for flavor.

Water Kettle

Coffee Grinder

Coffee Pot

∽❦ BAKING YEAST ❦∽

*I*f Grandma didn't have ingredients she needed in her cooking, she concocted them through trial and error. This yeast is a good example. Said she learned not to make it and put it out to dry during April's showers or August's rainy dog days.

FIREPLACE RECIPE:

Pick a double-handful of peach tree leaves, tie them in a cloth, and put it in a pan of boiling water. With this, put 1 or 2 good-size Irish potatoes cut up, and cover all with water. Cook until potatoes are done. Discard leaves and save juice.

Run potatoes through fine sieve and add enough juice back to make a pint. To this put enough cornmeal to form a stiff dough then roll out thin and cut into small squares, all the same size.

Dry thoroughly in the sun until hard, turning often. Store in dry place and use as needed.

A quick way, but has to be made often: When making biscuits, tear off a handful of dough, and put it in a pint fruit jar and cover it with water. Leave several days. Do not cover. Stir and use a half-pint to a quart of flour or if in a hurry for the rising, use more.

MODERN METHOD:

Nowadays we don't need to prepare this, because most grocery stores have active dry yeast available in airtight packages of 1 scant tablespoon or ¼ ounce. Most recipes refer to this size package.

TO WARM A CARRIAGE, OR SMALL APARTMENT

Convey into it a stone bottle of boiling water or for the feet a single glass bottle of boiled water wrapped in flannel.

—From *Mackenzie's Five Thousand Receipts* (1852)

COCOA-NUT BREAD

*G*randma declared Cousin Gussie did her best cooking when she was mad as a red-striped snake. One day Gussie purchased two items from the man at the medicine show: Sweet Mouth Gargle and Horse Liniment. When she got home, her taster discovered both bottles had come from the same pot, so she slung her cow-poking stick into the buggy and raced old Maude back to town to return them. Sadly, she found only wagon tracks. Back home, her frustration turned out the best batch of Cocoa-Nut Bread she ever made.

FIREPLACE RECIPE:

Pour 8 ounces of the finely rasped cocoa-nut into a quart of fresh milk. Heat slowly and simmer over coals very gently for a short hour; then take from the fire and when cooled, strain through a fine sieve or cloth.

Use the new milk while it is still warm, with yeast, good flour, lard, salt, a little sugar and a smidgen of honey as for common bread and manage it in exactly the same manner and bake as usual.

MODERN METHOD:

2¼ cups milk	2 tablespoons sugar
½ cup grated fresh coconut	1 tablespoon honey
1 package active dry yeast	2 tablespoons melted shortening
1¾ teaspoons salt	6 cups sifted all-purpose flour

Mix the milk and raw coconut in a saucepan and simmer over low heat 30 minutes. Cool and strain through a cloth. Apply pressure to gain full strength of the liquid. Cool to lukewarm. To ½ cup of the liquid, add the yeast and set aside.

In a large bowl, mix the remaining liquid with the salt, sugar, honey, and shortening. Add the yeast mixture. Blend in the flour gradually to make a stiff dough. Turn out on lightly floured board and knead until smooth and elastic. Place in a greased bowl, lightly grease the top, cover with a damp cloth, and let rise until doubled in bulk.

Turn the dough and punch it down. Shape into two loaves, and place in two 9 x 5-inch greased loaf tins. Cover with a damp cloth and let rise again until doubled in bulk.

Preheat the oven to 450° and bake the loaves 10 minutes. Reduce the heat to 350° and bake 25 to 30 minutes more, or until the bread shrinks from the sides of the pan and tests done with a toothpick. If baking in glass, reduce the heat by 50°. Cool on racks. *Makes 2 (1-pound) loaves.*

GEORGIA POTATO BREAD

*C*ousin Pearl poured a highly touted concoction of warm kerosene and washing powder on her hound dog to rid him of fleas. He died the next day. Grandma soothed her "what-ifs" by sending her a loaf of tender Georgia Potato Bread and a round of freshly churned butter topped with a rose print from her favorite butter mold.

FIREPLACE RECIPE:

Scrub potatoes thoroughly clean and boil not quite soft and dry at the hearth. Peel while hot and pound fine as possible for a half-pint, then put in sauce pan with a quart of liquid from boiling. Dissolve a suitable quantity of pearl ash* to new yeast. While it is working, add a hickory nut size chunk of butter melted, a stir-spoon of sugar and proper salt. After mixed, put in yeast then half the flour, about 3 tea-cups, and beat all together smooth. Add remaining flour and knead. Let dough stand in slight warmth before putting to the oven. It will not require so long baking as regular flour bread.

MODERN METHOD:

1 envelope active dry yeast	1 plus $1/2$ teaspoons salt
$1/2$ cup cooked, mashed potatoes (about 2 medium raw potatoes)	2 tablespoons butter or margarine, melted
2 cups warm water or potato liquid from boiling potatoes	3 to $3^{1}/2$ cups all-purpose flour

Dissolve the yeast in $1/2$ cup warm water and set aside to proof. Peel and cube the potatoes and place in a 2-quart saucepan. Cover with water, add $1/2$ teaspoon of the salt, and cook over medium heat until tender. Drain, saving the liquid. Mash the potatoes while hot. Add enough warm water to the liquid from the potatoes to make 2 cups. To this add the butter, the remaining 1 teaspoon salt and the softened yeast. Mix thoroughly, add half the flour, beat until smooth, and add the remaining flour gradually.

*Potassium carbonate from wood ashes.

Knead the dough on a floured board until soft and elastic. Place in a medium-size greased bowl, cover with a damp cloth, and set in warm place to rise. When doubled in bulk, divide and shape the dough into two loaves, and place in greased 9 x 5-inch loaf pans. Let rise again.

Preheat the oven to 375° and bake for 40 to 50 minutes or until the bread shrinks from the sides of the pan. *Makes 2 (1-pound) loaves.*

TETTER*, RINGWORM, AND BARBER'S ITCH—TO CURE

Take the best Cuba cigars, smoke one a sufficient length of time to accumulate ½ or ¼ inch of ashes upon the end of the cigar; now wet the whole surface of the sore with the saliva from the mouth, then rub the ashes from end of the cigar thoroughly into, and all over the sore; do this three times a day and inside of a week all will be smooth and well. I speak from extensive experience; half of one cigar cured myself when a barber would not undertake to shave me. It is equally successful in tetters on other parts of the body, hands, &c.

—From *Dr. Chase's Recipes* (1867)

*Psoriasis, herpes, eczema, and other skin conditions.

⤎ ETHY'S KIDNEY-BEAN BREAD ⤏

*T*all, raw-boned Cousin Ethy was a good-hearted old maid who loved to eat but never learned to cook. She collected recipes and often brought Grandma a new one. This was one of Ethy's favorites.

FIREPLACE RECIPE:

Take half-pint mashed pulp of kidney beans, add to it a small lump of lard, an egg or two, the common portion of yeast and mix all together. Put to this a short pint of flour with a little more salt than usual, a smidgen of cornmeal and a heavy dash of ground red pepper. Along with the mixing, add a little onion, a few parsley leaves, and a little fresh basil, all cut fine.

Knead same till spongy, put to rise, then bake over medium low coals an hour or more until done.

MODERN METHOD:

$\frac{1}{2}$ pound dry kidney beans	1 teaspoon salt
1 package active dry yeast	$\frac{1}{4}$ teaspoon ground red pepper
$\frac{1}{4}$ cup oil	$\frac{1}{4}$ cup finely chopped onion
2 eggs, beaten	1 tablespoon chopped parsley
$1\frac{3}{4}$ cups all-purpose flour, divided	1 tablespoon chopped basil
1 tablespoon cornmeal	Flour for kneading

Soak the beans in water overnight. The next morning, place the yeast in a separate small bowl and all $\frac{1}{2}$ cup warm water to dissolve. Drain the beans and in fresh water, boil until tender. Drain. While warm, run the beans through a strainer to divest them of skins.

Preheat the oven to 350°. In a large mixing bowl, place the oil and eggs, mix well, and blend in the yeast. Add the bean pulp. Gradually stir in half the flour sifted with the cornmeal, salt, and pepper. When smooth, add the onions, parsley, and basil; then mix in the balance of the flour gradually.

Turn the dough onto a floured board, and knead until smooth and elastic. Place in a greased 9 x 5-inch loaf pan, cover with a cloth, and let double in bulk. Bake about an hour or until the sides shrink from the pan and a knife inserted in the center comes out clean. Remove and cool on a rack. *Makes 1 medium-size loaf for 8 servings.*

❧ SUNDAY PUMPKIN BREAD ❧

*G*randma cooked all day every Saturday for Sunday's midday dinner, the celebrated meal of the week when the table overflowed with various foods. Many dishes came from the same basic ingredient, but each was different. From the lowly pumpkin came spiced dressing for pork shoulder or fowl, as well as jam, muffins, cookies, cake, custard pie, and this delicious bread.

FIREPLACE RECIPE:

Work a quarter pint of rich, fresh butter to a cream then put in three-quarters pound of finest sugar. Beat the whites of two eggs quarter of an hour and mix with the butter and sugar. Then beat the yolks for half an hour and put them to the butter. Beat the whole together and put to it a half pint of pumpkin, fresh cooked and mashed, a short pint of flour, seasoned, and sifted with gratings of a nutmeg ball and stick of cinnamon and a few heavy pinches of soda. When it is ready for the oven, mix in two good handfuls of broken hickory nut meats.

MODERN METHOD:

$1^3/_4$ cups sugar		$^3/_4$	teaspoon salt
$^1/_2$	cup vegetable oil	1	teaspoon baking soda
2	eggs, beaten	$^1/_2$	teaspoon nutmeg
1	cup canned pumpkin	$^1/_2$	teaspoon cinnamon
$1^3/_4$ cups all-purpose flour		$^1/_2$	cup chopped walnuts

Preheat the oven to 350°. In a large mixing bowl, place the sugar, oil, and eggs. Blend together and add the pumpkin. In another bowl, sift the flour, salt, soda, nutmeg, and cinnamon. Add the sifted dry ingredients to the egg mixture a little at a time, stirring well after each addition. Add the nuts. Pour into greased 9 x 5-inch loaf pan. Bake for 55 to 60 minutes. Test with a thin knife. Remove from the heat and set on a rack 10 minutes before turning out. *Makes 1 loaf for 8 servings.*

VARIATIONS: For *Squash Bread*, replace the pumpkin with squash. Any squash can be used, but winter squash is best. Boil, drain, and purée. Almonds may be added instead of walnuts.

For *Sweet Potato Bread*, replace the pumpkin with sweet potatoes. Boil the potatoes or yams, mash well after drained, and add back a little of the potato water so the mixture is the consistency of canned pumpkin. Pecan nuts add a smoother flavor than walnuts.

❧ FLAPJACKS ❧

*F*lapjacks served with Fried Syrup (see page 114) and hickory-smoked ham was one of the quickest meals Grandma could put together. She often prepared it for unexpected company or on washday when she was tired from boiling clothes in the black pot and pumping water for the three hand-rinses and wringings she did before hanging them on the line.

FIREPLACE RECIPE:

Stir well together a half-pint flour, one-fourth that of cornmeal, a little salt, a spoon of sugar and proper baking powder. Put to this a half-pint new milk, keep stirring till a smooth mass forms. Beat in one well-whipped egg, then a small lump of butter melted. Mix smooth and spoon batter onto very hot griddle pan to make desired-size flapjacks. Brown both sides, turning only once and send to the table hot. Serve with fried syrup and smokehouse ham.

MODERN METHOD:

1	cup flour	1	teaspoon baking powder
1/4	cup cornmeal	1	cup milk
1/2	teaspoon salt	1	egg, well beaten
1	tablespoon sugar	1	tablespoon butter, melted

Sift together the flour, cornmeal, salt, sugar, and baking powder. Stir in the milk. Add the egg and butter. Beat the mixture smooth and spoon the batter onto a hot, greased griddle. When brown on bottom, about 3 or 4 minutes, turn and brown the other side. Turn only once. If thinner cakes are desired, add a little more milk. Serve hot with Fried Syrup (see page 114), with or without ham or bacon. *Makes 10 (6-inch) flapjacks.*

⊱ BREAKFAST ICE CREAM ⊰

*G*randma confessed that when she and Grandpa were "spark-ing," she invited him to breakfast one morning. He bragged on her Breakfast Ice Cream so much, she was sure that's what won his heart.

FIREPLACE RECIPE:

Pour pint of sweet cream into saucepan and half cup of grits, pinch of salt, and cook over medium heat until thick, with a stir now and then. When done, dash in a little butter. Take to table hot for eggs, or cold with cream and sugar, or plain with rum sauce: boil sugar, lemon rind, lemon juice, thickening flour, a pinch of salt. Cool. Add rum to taste.

MODERN METHOD:

2 cups cream or half-and-half	$\frac{1}{2}$ cup quick grits
$\frac{1}{2}$ teaspoon salt	Rum Sauce (optional, recipe follows)

Mix the cream and salt and place over medium heat. Bring to a boil and slowly stir in the grits. Bring to a boil again, reduce the heat, cover, and cook 5 to 8 minutes until thick, stirring occasionally. Serve hot or cold with Rum Sauce or with cream or milk and sugar. *Makes 2 large servings.*

Rum Sauce

1 cup sugar	$\frac{1}{8}$ teaspoon salt
$1\frac{1}{3}$ tablespoons grated lemon rind	3 tablespoons lemon juice
$1\frac{1}{2}$ cups boiling water	1 tablespoon butter, melted
1 teaspoon flour	$\frac{1}{2}$ cup rum
2 tablespoons cornstarch	

In a double boiler, mix the sugar and lemon rind with the boiling water, and place over a container of boiling water. When the mix is well heated, not boiling, remove and cool. Blend in the flour, cornstarch, and salt. Stir in the lemon juice and butter, and again place over the boiling water. Cook 7 to 8 minutes or until as thick as pudding and remove from the heat. Add the rum. Serve hot. *Makes about 2 cups.*

∾ MUSCADINE GRITS ∾

*A*unt Viola was not going fishing when she traipsed across the field to the woods with her cane fishing pole over her shoulder and a bucket swinging in her hand. She was on her way to beat muscadine grapes from vines in the trees to flavor grits.

FIREPLACE RECIPE:

In a goodly amount of chicken stock, cook a handful of pulp from muscadines already hulled and seeded. Add as much grits as it takes to make a firm mush. When done, drop in a dollop of fresh churned butter, a pinch of salt, and a dash or two of pepper. Sprinkle top with pieces of parched pecans. Eat while hot.

May top with dash of grape catsup: Place in patty pan grapes, sugar, spices as liked, a dash of flour and vinegar. Put pan in Dutch Oven with finger of water. Cook over hot coals and stir till thickened. Sieve.

MODERN METHOD:

1 cup seedless green grapes, washed and quartered	$1^1/_4$ tablespoons butter
	$^1/_4$ teaspoon black pepper
4 cups chicken broth, fresh or canned	$^1/_2$ cup Parched (Toasted) Pecans
1 cup uncooked grits	(see page 190), coarsely chopped
$^1/_2$ teaspoon salt, or to taste	

Combine the grapes and chicken broth. Boil briskly 15 to 20 minutes or until the grape skins are fairly tender. Continue boiling and add the grits and salt (note that pecans are slightly salty). Cook 6 to 8 minutes longer to thickness desired. Quick grits may take less time. A little water can be added. Remove from the heat and add the butter and black pepper. Take the grits up in a serving dish and sprinkle the top with the pecans. Fine with any fowl. *Makes 6 servings.*

NOTE: These grits are good for chicken or turkey stuffing—use double the amount of nuts. If making for turkey stuffing, use turkey stock. A little Grape Catsup (see page 128) adds to the flavor.

Poultry, Meats, Fish, and Eggs

CHIEF'S CHICKEN

*G*randma visited her Cherokee fourth cousin, Mahalia, to get an herbal cure for a stomach ailment. She went home with two remedies to make the stomach happy, the second being this chicken, an Indian recipe using nuts named "pecans" by our Indian ancestors.

FIREPLACE RECIPE:

Dress a plump hen: remove and throw out lungs, kidneys, windpipe, crop, and oil bag at base of tail. Wash well inside and out. Place in large kettle with half gallon of water and adequate salt, top and boil over mid fire till tender, and having half of the water.

While it cooks, heat egg-size lump of butter in spider pan and fry to a golden brown, a quarter-pint of pecan bits, a sweet onion sliced, a handful of dried sweet grapes seed out, a stick of cinnamon and a clove or two. Remove this from pan and in same butter fry a full tea-cup of raw rice till golden brown, drain, and add with a dash or two of flour and all other to kettle of chicken. Boil till chicken and rice both are nice tender. Place the whole handsomely on a dish and frame with bits of tender dandelion or other greens.

MODERN METHOD:

1 (4 to 5-pound) stewing hen, dressed	$1/4$ cup raisins
2 quarts water with $1^{1}/_2$ teaspoons salt for boiling	2 cloves
	$1/4$ teaspoon cinnamon
$1/2$ cup butter or margarine	$1^{1}/_4$ cups raw rice
$1/2$ cup raw pecans, chopped	1 tablespoon flour
1 medium-size sweet onion, sliced	Parsley and celery sticks for garnish

In a deep, heavy pot, cover the hen with the salted water. Over a low heat, boil the chicken until tender, 2 to 4 hours, depending on its age. Add water if needed to make a quart of broth. Skim off the grease and discard.

While the chicken cooks, place in a frying pan the butter, pecans, onion, raisins, cloves, and cinnamon. Slow-fry the ingredients until brown, stirring constantly. Remove them from the pan, leaving 1 tablespoon butter. In this butter, fry the rice until brown, stirring to prevent scorching. Drain. Blend a little of the broth from the chicken with the flour, and add back to the chicken with the rice and fried ingredients. Taste for seasoning. Cook until the rice is tender and the chicken falls from the bones. Remove the bones, cut the chicken in pieces, and place the chicken and rice on separate platters. Extra liquid, if any, can be used for gravy. Garnish with parsley and celery sticks. Serve hot. *Makes 10 servings.*

RENOVATING MIXTURES

For Grease Spots, Shampooing, and Killing Bed-Bugs. Aqua ammonia 2 ozs; soft water 1 qt.; salt petre 1 tea-spoon, variegated shaving soap 1 oz., or one 3 cent cake, finely shaved or scraped; mix all, shake well, and it will be a little better to stand a few hours or days before using, which gives the soap a chance to dissolve.

Directions.—Pour upon the place a sufficient amount to well cover any grease or oil which may get spilled or daubed upon coats, pants, carpets, &c., sponging and rubbing well and applying again if necessary to saponify the grease in the garment; then wash off with clear cold water.

Don't squirm now, for these are not half it will do—some people fly entirely off the handle when a preparation is said to do many things—for my part, however, I always admire an article in proportion to the labor which can be performed by it or with it.

This preparation will shampoo like a charm; raising the lather in proportion to the amount of grease and dandruff in the hair. It will remove paint, even from a board, I care not how long it has been applied, if oil was used in the paint—and yet it does not injure the finest textures, for the simple reason that its affinity is for grease or oil, changing them to soap, and thus loosening any substance with which they may be combined.

If it is put upon a bed-bug he will never step afterwards, and if put into their crevices, it destroys their eggs and thus drives them from the premises.

A cloth wet with it will soon remove all the grease and dirt from doors which are much opened by kitchen-hands.

—From *Dr. Chase's Recipes* (1867)

45

❦ CHICKEN AND ❦
CLOUD-TENDER DUMPLIN'S

*G*randma always saved the fat when she boiled a chicken. She skimmed it from the top of the pot to use for ailments. One use was mixing it with mashed valerian leaves to cure toe corns.

FIREPLACE RECIPE:

Place a fat hen dressed and properly cleaned in Dutch oven or hanging pot after it is disjointed, and barely cover with salted water. Simmer slow until meat falls from bones. Remove from fire, skim and save fat; take out undesirables. Remove chicken from broth. Set aside.

Make dumplings with a pint of flour having proper baking powder and salt, add an egg-size lump of shortening and with a fork, make same into crumbs. Proceed for a stiff dough with a little milk and roll on floured board to less than $1/4$ biscuit thickness. Cut in short strips with sharp knife, flour good, and shake off surplus.

Put Dutch oven with chicken broth back to fire rather hot, and when at full boil, fast drop each strip into liquid and quickly cover pot. Simmer slow about 40 minutes.

Do not peek. Keep top closed tight or dumplings will fall.

MODERN METHOD:

Chicken

1   (4-pound) stewing chicken, cleaned and disjointed
1   teaspoon salt

Place the chicken in a heavy pot, and fill with enough water to cover, about $1\frac{1}{2}$ quarts. Add the salt. Boil the chicken until the meat is very tender. Remove from the heat and reserve the chicken broth for cooking the dumplings. Place the chicken on a plate, and when cool, remove the skin and bones, cover, and keep warm. Reheat before serving.

Dumplings

2 cups all-purpose flour	$1/4$ cup shortening
2 teaspoons baking power	$1/2$ cup plus 1 tablespoon milk
$1/2$ teaspoon salt	Reserved chicken broth (see above)

Sift the flour, baking powder, and salt together, and cut in the shortening until the particles are no bigger than peas. Add the milk and knead to a stiff dough. Roll out on a floured board to $1/4$-inch thickness, and cut with a sharp knife into 1 x 2-inch strips. Shake off the surplus flour.

Place the pot of reserved broth on the heat and bring to a rolling boil. There should be about a quart of liquid. A little water may be added. Keep a rolling boil, and hurriedly drop the dough strips into the liquid, one at a time, closing the lid after each addition to let as little steam escape as possible. Cover tightly and simmer over low heat 40 minutes. During this time do not open the lid. Air will make the dumplings fall. Serve piping hot in a separate dish along with the reheated chicken. *Makes 8 to 10 servings*.

CARING FOR FIREPLACE COOKWARE

New cast-iron pots had to be seasoned (seared) before use. This was done by coating the inside with lard and placing the pot over a very hot, but waning, fire for at least an hour. The pot smoked profusely, a signal that meant the job was being done properly. When the pot was cold, it was wiped with a clean cloth and was ready for use.

After cooking, the pots were not washed with soap and water; rather, food was scraped out and the pot wiped clean with a rag greased with lard. If soap and water was absolutely necessary, the pot had to be reseasoned to prevent sticking. When the outside of the pot accumulated a buildup of soot, it was scoured with straw from the barn and sand from the yard.

❧ PREACHER'S CHICKEN DINNER ❧

*A*unt Hattie Mae thrived on raves for her cooking. Instead of serving the usual fried chicken to the preacher one Sunday, she put on her thinking cap and came up with this goody. Needless to say, she got the raves and "God bless you's" she deserved.

FIREPLACE RECIPE:

Make a batch of noodles with flour, a little salt, a whole fresh-laid egg frothed, and enough milk to make a stiff dough. Roll out very thin, cut in narrow strips, and let same dry in sun until can handle separately. May take a few sunnings.

Cut up a hen dressed and drawn, dip pieces in frothed egg, flour, put in spider pan with hot grease and fry brown. Remove chicken to kettle with about 2 quarts of water and boil until tender. Save broth. To this put a spoon of salt, a half-dozen red-ripe tomatoes, peeled, half-pint sweet onions, some bell pepper, carrot, and parsley to suit, all cut fine, a little lemon juice, a dash of red pepper powder or fine grated. Boil this, put in noodles, cook till tender. Send to table steaming hot.

MODERN METHOD:

1	(4 to 5-pound) stewing chicken, cut up	1/2	cup diced bell pepper
1	egg, beaten	1/2	cup small-cubed carrots
1/2	cup flour for dredging	1	tablespoon chopped parsley
	Oil for frying	1	teaspoon lemon juice
1 1/4	teaspoons salt	1/2	teaspoon cayenne
	Drippings from frying	3	cups broken noodles
1	(15-ounce) can tomatoes		Parsley sprigs for garnish
1	cup diced sweet onions		

Dip the pieces of chicken in the egg, roll in the flour, and fry in hot oil until both sides brown. Save the drippings. Remove the chicken and place in a heavy pot with water to cover. Add the salt along with the drippings from frying and boil until tender. Should boil down to about a quart of broth. Add tomatoes, onions, pepper, carrots, parsley, lemon juice, and cayenne.

Boil 10 to 15 minutes over medium heat or until the carrots begin to tender. Taste for seasoning. Add the noodles and cook until tender, 8 to 10 minutes. If needed, add water, but sparingly, to preserve the hearty taste. When finished, the dish should have little juice. Bone the chicken. Serve the chicken, vegetables, and noodles together on a platter, or separately. Garnish with sprigs of parsley. Serve hot, preferably with biscuits. *Makes 8 servings*.

BRILLIANT STUCCO WHITEWASH

Will last on brick or stone twenty to thirty years.

Many have heard of the brilliant stucco whitewash on the east end of the President's house at Washington. The following is a recipe for it, as gleaned from the *National Intelligencer*.

Nice unslaked lime ½ bushel, slake it with boiling water; cover it during the process, to keep in the steam. Strain the liquid through a fine sleve or strainer, and add to it, salt 1 peck; previously well dissolved in water; rice 3 lbs.—boiled to a thin paste, and stirred in boiling hot; Spanish whiting ½ lb.; clean nice glue 1 lb., which has been previously dissolved by soaking it well, and then hanging it over a slow fire, in a small kettle, immersed in a larger one filled with water.

Now add hot water 5 gals, to the mixture, stir it well, and let it stand a few days covered from the dirt.

It should be put on hot. For this purpose it can be kept in a kettle on a portable furnace.

Brushes more or less small may be used, according to the neatness of job required. It answers as well as oil paint for brick or stone, and is much cheaper.

—From *Dr. Chase's Recipes* (1867)

∽ PICKLED CHICKEN ∽

*G*randma often took this dish to All-Day Singing and Dinner on the Ground at the church on the fourth Sunday. Since it was best served cold, she fixed it on Saturday and didn't sin by cooking on Sunday.

FIREPLACE RECIPE:

Take a large hen properly dressed and cut into joints. Roll each well in flour and brown quick in lard in Dutch oven over hot flame, careful not to scorch. Remove chicken and pour off most of fat. In remaining, fry gizzard and heart cut fine, 2 large sweet onions, sliced. Place all in kettle, cover over with water, add proper salt and pepper and drop in a faggot* of parsley and a sprig or two of thyme.

Cook over slow fire until chicken is tender, then put to it a half-pint cider vinegar and cook a half-hour more, or until pierced thigh proves tender. Remove chicken. Discard faggot. Boil broth to a pint and to it put equal amount of fine biscuit crumbs and cook shortly to a fine taste. Pour over chicken in a large dish. Serve after cooled or next day.

MODERN METHOD:

1 (4½ to 5-pound) chicken, including gizzard and heart	½ teaspoon black pepper Pinch of thyme
1 cup flour for dredging	10 sprigs parsley in bundle tied with sewing thread
½ cup oil for frying	
2 cups sliced sweet onions	1 cup cider vinegar, or to taste
1 teaspoon salt	2 cups stale breadcrumbs

Cut up the chicken. Chop the gizzard and heart and set aside. Dredge the chicken pieces in flour, and brown both sides quickly in hot oil in a heavy skillet. Remove. Drain and discard all but 2 tablespoons oil; in this oil, sauté the onions, gizzard, and heart. Place this mix and the chicken in a deep pot, and barely cover with water. Add the salt and pepper, thyme, and parsley, and bring to a boil. Lower the heat, and simmer 2 to 3 hours until the chicken

*A bundle tied together with thread or string.

is very tender. Remove the parsley. Add the vinegar. Cook at least 15 minutes more and remove from the heat. Remove the fat from the broth and cook the broth down to a pint.

Add the breadcrumbs, blend till smooth, and cook down to suit your taste. Add more seasonings as desired. Pour the mixture over the chicken placed on a large serving platter. This recipe may be prepared the day before use. It is best served cold. *Makes 8 servings*.

CANCERS—TO CURE

L. S. Hodgkins' Method.—This gentleman is a merchant of Reding, Mich. The method is not original with him, but he cured his wife with it, of cancer of the breast, after having been pronounced incurable. Some would use it because it contains calomel—others would not use it for the same reason. I give it an insertion from the fact that I am well satisfied that it has cured the disease, and from its singularity of composition.

Take a white oak root and bore out the heart and burn the chips to get the ashes 1/4 oz.; lunar caustic 1/4 oz; calomel 1/4 oz. salts of nitre (salt petre) 1/4 oz; the body of a thousand-legged worm, dried and pulverized, all to be made fine and mixed with 1/4 pound of lard.

Spread this rather thin upon soft leather, and apply to the Cancer, changing twice a day; will kill the tumor in three or four days, which you will know by the general appearance; then apply a poultice of soaked figs until it comes out, fibres and all; heal with a plaster made by boiling red beech leaves in water, straining and boiling thick, then mix with beeswax and mutton tallow to form a salve of proper consistency.

The juice of pokeberries, set in the sun, upon a pewter dish, and dried to a consistence of a salve, and applied as a plaster, has cured cancer.

Poultices of scraped carrots, and of yellow dock root, have cured cancer. . . .

Figs boiled in new milk until tender, then split and applied hot—changing twice daily, washing the parts every change, with some of the milk—drinking 1 gill of the milk also as often. And continuing from three to four months, is also reported to have cured a man of ninety-nine years old by using only six pounds, whilst ten pounds cured a case of ten years' standing. The first application giving pain, but afterwards relief, every application.

—From *Dr. Chase's Recipes* (1867)

51

⚮ AUNT SALLY'S HOT POT ⚮

*A*unt Sally bragged about her coaxing ways. The day before she wanted to take the horse and buggy to the general store to buy a new bonnet or dress cloth, she made Uncle Fred happy with this one-dish dinner accompanied by golden brown, finger-burning biscuits oozing butter from the middles. It never failed her.

FIREPLACE RECIPE:

Cut 2 pounds tender stew beef into pieces convenient for the bite. Peel ample potatoes for servings wanted and cut them into small, thick pieces; slice 4 egg size onions thin, let wait, a little flour and roll each piece of meat in the mixture.

Put a layer of potatoes in a heavy, deep dish or bowl (a wide-mouthed bean pot is satisfactory), then a layer of meat and next, the sliced onion, repeating the process till the dish is filled. Have potatoes for the last layer and then fill the dish with water or meat stock. Cover and set in Dutch oven. Bake three hours over moderate coals, adding more water if necessary. Serve hot.

MODERN METHOD:

2	pounds tender stew beef	1	teaspoon salt
6	medium-size potatoes	$3/4$	teaspoon chili powder
4	medium-size onions	2	cups meat stock or canned beef broth
$1/2$	cup all-purpose flour		

Preheat the oven to 350°. Cut the meat into bite-size pieces and the potatoes into $3/4$-inch cubes. Slice the onions thinly. Roll each piece of meat in a sifted mix of the flour, salt, and chili powder. In a 2-quart casserole, place a layer of potatoes, then meat, then onion. Repeat, with the last layer being potatoes. Sparsely cover the layers with meat stock. Cover and bake in the oven for 3 hours. Add more broth if necessary. Serve hot. *Makes 8 servings.*

⌒ TOAD IN THE HOLE ⌒

$\mathcal{G}$randma said she never fixed this dish when her three- and four-year-old grandchildren visited. They were afraid the toad would jump out and gobble them up.

FIREPLACE RECIPE:

Butter well a pudding dish, lay in it a piece of tender beefsteak, about a pound not too thick, and sprinkle same with salt and pepper, a potato or two grated, and a little chopped onion.

Beat up a fresh egg and put to this a half-pint of milk and same of self-rising flour. Stir well together. The mix should be smooth liken to that for batter cakes. Pour over meat and set in spider over medium coals on trivet. Cover and bake about an hour.

MODERN METHOD:

1 pound tender steak, about ¾-inch thick	1 cup all-purpose flour
½ plus ½ plus ¼ teaspoons salt	1 teaspoon baking powder
¼ teaspoon pepper	1 egg, beaten
1 cup grated potato	1 cup milk

Preheat the oven to 350°. Pound the steak to tenderize. Place it in the bottom of a greased 2-quart casserole. Sprinkle the steak with ½ teaspoon salt mixed with the pepper, and cover with the grated potato, mixed with ¼ teaspoon salt.

In a medium-size bowl, sift the flour with the baking powder and the remaining ½ teaspoon salt. In a smaller bowl, mix the egg with the milk, and add a little at a time to the flour mixture, stirring until smooth after each addition. Batter will be thin. Spoon the egg mixture over the steak in the casserole, taking care not to disturb the layer of potatoes. Bake 50 minutes to 1 hour or until brown and a toothpick stuck near the center comes out clean. Remove from the oven. Cut in wedges and serve with a spatula. *Makes 4 servings.*

MEATBALLS AND SQUASH WITH CORN PATTIES

The inside of Grandma's chinked log smokehouse looked like a meat market with its hams, ribs, fatback, and ropes of sausage hanging about. Her choice for the day's meals was always waiting a few steps from her back door.

FIREPLACE RECIPE:

Roll a pound of seasoned pork sausage into balls of thumb-size and fry a nice brown in spider pan. When done, take up, drain, and let wait. Have food chopper ready.

Take a pint of squash, crookneck or patty-pan, and grind coarse in food chopper with a half dozen red-ripe tomatoes and a large onion.

Grind fresh hot red peppers trimmed and seeded, of a quarter-dozen; reduce for those of ill health. Put all grindings and a pinch of salt in the oil-drained spider pan, set on trivet over simmer coals until squash is about tender. To this put sausage balls and slow cook a little time. Set aside until cold to allow seasoning to strike through. Reheat and pour into warm bowl to spoon over corn patties.

Make patties with a pint of buttermilk, a little warmed butter, proper salt, rising, and eggs, and to this put cornmeal, about a pint, for a medium batter. Dissolve proper soda in a dribble of cold water and stir into the whole.

Drop dough 2 or 3 spoonfuls onto hot, greased griddle pan. Cakes should be thin and spread to palm-size; if too thick, add milk. Brown both sides, turning once. Stack as flapjacks and take to table hot.

Eaters spoon meatballs and squash over same.

MODERN METHOD:

Meatballs

1 pound seasoned pork sausage (if spicy, omit red pepper)

2 cups tender squash, crookneck or summer, cut in 2-inch cubes

1 1/2 cups chopped ripe tomatoes, about 6

1 cup finely chopped onions

1 teaspoon hot red peppers, seeded and deveined, finely puréed in blender (optional)

1/2 teaspoon salt

1/4 cup water

Roll the sausage into marble-size balls. Fry them brown in a small frying pan. Drain.

In a medium-size saucepan, place the squash, tomatoes, and onions. Add the red peppers and salt to the water, and blend into the vegetable mix. Slow-simmer until the squash bits are done but still slightly crunchy, 12 to 15 minutes, depending on the squash. Add the sausage balls, bring to a boil, and quickly turn down the heat. Simmer another 3 minutes. Set aside until cold, giving flavors time to mingle, and then reheat before serving.

Corn Patties

2	cups cornmeal	1	teaspoon baking soda
1/4	cup all-purpose flour	2	cups buttermilk
1 1/4	teaspoons salt	2	eggs, well beaten
1 1/2	teaspoons baking powder	2	tablespoons butter or margarine, melted

Mix together the cornmeal, flour, salt, baking powder, and soda. Gradually add the buttermilk. Mix well. Blend in the eggs and butter.

Drop by spoonfuls onto a hot, well-greased griddle. Should flatten to about 1/3 inch by 6 inches. Should be thin. If too thick, add a little milk. Will be thicker when done. Brown the bottom, then the top, turning once. Several may be placed on a large grill at the same time.

Stack as pancakes, and serve at once with reheated meatballs and the squash mixture spooned on top as syrup. *Makes 6 servings.*

↝ COUNTRY SAUSAGES ↜

*M*onday was washday. Grandma boiled clothes in the big black wash pot, took out each steaming piece with an oar-like battle stick, and beat out the dirt on a battling block, a stump beaten smooth. Once the clothes were clean and sterile, she hand-wrung them through three rinse waters. Dinners and suppers on those days were scant, but she made up for them next day with these sausages served with Pease Pudding (see page 69).

FIREPLACE RECIPE:

Take short pound of young lean pork, same of lean veal, and same of beef suet. Chop fine together. Put in a short pint of stale biscuit crumbs, shredded peel of half a lemon, 8 or 10 sage leaves chopped fine, a tea-spoonful of salt, pepper to taste.

Mix well together and mash close down in the pan till used. Make rounds the size of common sausages, roll in a little flour and fry in fresh butter, of a fine brown, or broil them over a clear fire and send to the table hot.

Especially good served with Pease Pudding.

MODERN METHOD:

$3/4$ pound pork
$3/4$ pound veal
$1/2$ pound beef suet
$1^1/2$ cups stale breadcrumbs
2 tablespoons water

$3/4$ teaspoon grated lemon rind
1 teaspoon ground sage
$1^1/2$ teaspoons salt
$1/4$ teaspoon black pepper
Butter for frying

Very finely grind the pork, veal, and suet. Moisten the breadcrumbs with the water and mix with the meat. Add the lemon rind, sage, salt, and black pepper and mix thoroughly.

Make a firm ball of the mix, and with a rolling pin, roll out on a sparsely floured board to a circle about $3/4$ inch in diameter. Cut into 2- to 3-inch lengths.

Fry in shallow butter in a covered pan over low heat 10 to 12 minutes until done and brown on each side. Serve hot. Good with Pease Pudding (see page 69). *Makes about 2 dozen sausages.*

CRAWDAD DUMPLIN'S

*G*randma said she seldom served crawdads because she didn't have any. Folks kept them "caught up" and didn't throw back the babies to grow to keepers. But she often sang the "Crawdad Song" while Grandpa strummed the guitar.

FIREPLACE RECIPE:

Take 2 or 3 dozen crawdads, as many as caught, and clean from all grit. Throw away heads and tail swimmer fins. Let wait.

Cover crawdads with water in boiling pot. To this put a large onion, chopped, 3 green onion tops chopped; celery seed, a heavy spoonful; parsley, several sprigs chopped fine; hot pepper pod, about a half chopped fine, or as wished. Salt to taste. Simmer over low fire until onions mush, strain and mash all together as paste and let wait as sauce. Put crawfish in liquid from straining, boil tender, take up, and keep warm.

Cook dumplings in liquid, add water if needed, put a little juice to paste and pour over top of crawdads in separate dish. Serve all hot.

MODERN METHOD:

The same basic recipe is used today. See Dumplings recipe on page 47. *Makes 8 to 10 servings.*

DESTROY ANTS

Wash shelves where they congregate with strong alum water, scatter sprigs of sweet fern, pennyroyal, or pieces of alum there. . . . Apply alum water strong and hot to everyplace where there are insects or vermin and it will kill them.

—From *The Housekeeper Cook Book* (1894)

AUNT HATTIE MAE'S SATURDAY CATFISH

Aunt Hattie had the reputation of always serving dinner at noon sharp, except on mornings when the fish were not hungry. On those days, she had to sit longer on the bank throwing back the little fish. When she caught enough keepers and finished cleaning and cooking them, dinner was always late.

FIREPLACE RECIPE:

Take a half-dozen thick slabs from just-caught catfish, properly cleaned, free of bones, roll same in cornmeal, salt, pepper. Give a quick brown crust to both sides in sizzling grease in spider pan. Drain grease.

In cooking pan, make 2 layers of thus: lay fish in bottom, onto this lay thick slices of red-ripe tomatoes, salted properly. Onto this, throw onion chopped to bits along with equal parts of dill and parsley leaves fine cut together. Repeat with all.

Over the whole pour thin corn pastry of a little flour in 2 handfuls of meal properly seasoned, a fresh egg mixed with buttermilk, soda, and a little butter. Bake with a few coals in lid until of proper color. Send to the table with a dish of fresh-made horseradish sauce.

For good smooth horseradish sauce, best cooked over water in Dutch oven. Put to a saucepan melted butter, a little flour, and stir smooth. To this put fresh milk slowly so as to blend, season with salt and pepper, add egg yolk, stir till bubbling. Let stay a few minutes till thickened. Remove from fire, put in desired amount of fresh horseradish root, scraped and grated fine, and mix. Serve with catfish dish.

MODERN METHOD:

6 catfish fillets, about 1 1/2 pounds
1/2 cup cornmeal for dredging
1/2 teaspoon salt
1/4 teaspoon pepper
1/3 cup oil for frying
1 1/2 cups ripe tomatoes, thinly sliced and salted to taste

1/2 cup finely chopped onion
1/4 teaspoon dill seed or 1 tablespoon fresh dill leaves, chopped
1 tablespoon finely chopped parsley
Cornmeal Topping (recipe follows)
Horseradish Sauce (recipe follows)

Preheat the oven to 425°. Dredge the fish in the cornmeal mixed with the salt and pepper. Quickly brown the fish in hot oil in a deep, ovenproof skillet (to be thoroughly cooked later). Remove and discard the oil.

Divide the fish and the other ingredients into two equal parts for two layers. For the first layer, half the fish in the bottom of a buttered 2-quart casserole, add half the tomato slices, and sprinkle with half the onion, dill, and parsley. For the second layer, add the remaining fish, tomato slices, onion, dill, and parsley. Pour the Cornmeal Topping over the top. Using a knife, cut 5 or 6 channels down the inside edges of the casserole, and let some of the topping run down the channels. Smooth out the top.

Bake in the oven for 15 to 18 minutes or until golden brown. Serve hot with fresh Horseradish Sauce. *Makes 8 servings.*

Cornmeal Topping

$1^1/4$ cups cornmeal	$1/2$ teaspoon baking soda
2 tablespoons flour	1 cup buttermilk
2 teaspoons baking powder	1 egg, well beaten
$1/2$ teaspoon salt	2 tablespoons butter, melted

Sift the cornmeal, flour, baking powder, salt, and soda together; add the buttermilk. Blend in the egg and butter and mix thoroughly.

Horseradish Sauce

1 tablespoon flour	2 tablespoons butter or margarine, melted
2 teaspoons cornstarch	1 teaspoon lemon juice
$1^1/2$ cups milk	4 level teaspoons prepared pure
1 egg yolk, beaten	horseradish, or to taste
	Salt and pepper

In the top of a double boiler, combine the flour and cornstarch. Blend in the milk. Add the egg yolk and butter. Place over boiling water. Cook until slightly thickened, stirring constantly. The mixture should be thin. Add the lemon juice. Cook 1 more minute and remove from the heat. Thoroughly mix in the prepared horseradish. Add the salt and pepper to taste.

AUNT GUSSIE'S COMPANY EGGS

*A*unt Gussie's was the place to be at mealtime. She cooked the plainest of foods into company fare, as you will see by these eggs. This is a fine dish for any meal, especially for breakfast with thick, golden brown, butter-dripping biscuits.

FIREPLACE RECIPE:

Cook a dozen eggs twenty minutes in water a little short of the boiling point, stand them in cold water for half an hour, then remove the shells and wipe the eggs quite dry.

Cook a half-pint of stale bread crumbs in hefty half-pint of rich milk until thick, add salt and pepper to taste. To this, add one pint cooked ground boiled ham and mix all together to form a rather stiff paste.

Take of this and press around one egg smoothly with the hand, having paste of equal thickness all over. Continue till all eggs are covered. Take a raw egg with a spoon of water, beat lightly, dip each of prepared eggs, and cover every particle. Drop onto paper containing stale bread crumbs. Fry in spider pan in sizzling fat over hot coals till golden brown. Cut in halves roundwise, stand cut side up and serve hot, either plain or with nasturtium gravy, or sawmill or gingersnap gravy.

MODERN METHOD:

6 hard-cooked eggs	1 raw egg
$1/2$ cup stale breadcrumbs for batter	1 teaspoon water
$2/3$ cup milk	$1/2$ cup fresh breadcrumbs for coating
Salt and pepper	Oil for frying
1 cup finely minced boiled ham	$1/8$ teaspoon paprika (optional)

Peel and dry the hard-cooked eggs. Cook the $1/2$ cup stale breadcrumbs and milk to a thick batter; add the salt and pepper. Mix in the dry ham to form a stiff paste. With your hand, press one-sixth of this paste smoothly around the first boiled egg, keeping the thickness equal. Lay the egg gently on a paper towel, and continue coating until all the eggs are covered.

Beat the raw egg and water together lightly. Dip each of the prepared eggs into this, covering every particle. Place each egg in the fresh breadcrumbs and roll to completely coat. With a slotted spoon, ease the eggs one by one into deep, hot fat, keeping them separated, and cook briefly until golden brown.

Cut the eggs in half, stand the cut side up in a bowl to fit, and sprinkle the top with paprika. Serve hot, either plain or with gravy. Try it with Nasturtium Gravy, Sawmill Gravy, or Gingersnap Gravy (see pages 100, 102, and 104). *Makes 6 servings.*

THE ICE HOUSE

Ice, the great luxury of summer, has become a necessity, and though the cities seem to have an advantage because of the quantity stored for general use, yet it is so easily put up and protected even in the country, there is no reason why anyone who owns or rents a house may not have a good supply.

A place twelve or fifteen feet square can be partitioned off in the barn or wood-house. The roof must be tight. A coat of coal-tar should be laid on inside walls, as the moisture will cause decay. The house should always be kept closed, as the darker it is, and the less circulation of air, the better the ice will keep.

The best time to cut ice is on a sharp, cold day in early winter, as it will keep much better through the long, hot summer than if packed in late winter, or early spring. Cut the ice from running streams or clear ponds, and have the blocks uniform in size. Place sawdust a foot thick under the first layer of ice, leaving a space a foot wide between the ice and the wall, in which pack sawdust, filling every crevice.

An ice-plow or saw can be obtained in almost any village for the purpose of cutting ice. An old cross-cut saw is sometimes used, and answers very well.

—From *The Housekeeper Cook Book* (1894)

⮾ ORANGE OMELET ⮿

*L*ong before Hollywood became known as the glamour capital, Grandma's sister Hattie personified a movie star. Before she came to the kitchen to make morning coffee, she brushed and bunned her sleek brown hair, put Sunday powder on her face, and donned a starched and flawlessly ironed apron. Grandma always made something special for her when she visited, like this omelet.

FIREPLACE RECIPE:

Take 3 oranges and remove seed and every particle of white pith; then break pulp into small pieces in its juice and add sugar to taste and set up to mellow.

Take yolks of 6 fresh-laid eggs, beat in a little water and a smidgen of salt, and put together with the whites whipped stiff. Heat a walnut-size lump of the best butter in a skillet and pour in eggs. Cook a slight minute on trivet over slack fire until omelet is set. Then cover pan and cook a short minute until top is firm to touch and of good color. Remove and spread a few pieces of the orange on the omelet; double it together quickly, and turn onto a hot dish. Strew remainder of orange around it and serve at once, as it soon falls.

MODERN METHOD:

2	oranges, medium size	$^1/_4$	teaspoon salt
2	tablespoons sugar for orange and juice, or to taste	4	eggs, separated
4	tablespoons warm water	2	tablespoons butter or margarine

Peel the oranges. Ready the segments by removing the dividers and seeds; sprinkle with the sugar. Set in a warm place to mellow until the omelet is done.

Preheat the oven to 400°. Add the water and salt to the egg yolks and beat well. Stiffly beat the egg whites and blend with the yolks. Heat the butter in an omelet pan, swishing to cover the sides, and pour in the eggs. Cook over moderate heat about a minute, until a spatula slid under the omelet indicates it is set. Place the pan on the upper rack of the oven, and cook another minute or until firm to touch and very slightly browned. Watch it carefully. If cooked too long, it will not be creamy in the center and will be tough.

Remove from the oven immediately and spread the orange segments on the omelet. Mark across the center with a knife and fold the two sides together quickly. Roll the omelet onto a hot dish, and pour the remaining orange segments around the sides. Serve at once. *Makes 2 servings.*

Vegetables

⤲ COMPANY CABBAGE ⤲

$\mathcal{G}$randma compared the swiftness of cooking this dish to the length of time the Turkey Trot dance stayed around her community when she was young. It was promptly outlawed because couples coiled and wiggled their bodies around in disgraceful gyrations like snakes trying to walk.

FIREPLACE RECIPE:

Put a quart of shredded cabbage in Dutch oven with a little melted fresh butter, a handful of beets cut fine, and cook a few minutes until limber. Easy to scorch. To this, put a peeled and coarsely chopped red apple, a little molasses, and juice of a lemon. Sprinkle all with a little salt and a few pinches of sugar. Place lid on without coals, and cook very slow until most crunch is gone.

MODERN METHOD:

4 cups cabbage, finely shredded, small head about 1 pound	$^1/_2$ cup sugarcane molasses
$^1/_2$ cup unpeeled, diced raw beets	3 tablespoons lemon juice
3 tablespoons butter or margarine	$^1/_2$ teaspoon salt
	1 cup coarsely chopped cooking apple

Combine the cabbage and beets in a heavy pot with the melted butter. Cook over medium-low heat 8 to 10 minutes, stirring constantly, until the cabbage is soft. Add the molasses, lemon juice, and salt. Cover and simmer over lowest heat, stirring often. After simmering 15 minutes, add the apple and cook about 10 more minutes or until the apple has a slight crunch, but is not mushy. Serve hot. *Makes 6 servings*.

⌒ CABBAGE PUDDING ⌒

*G*randpa stayed in the barn, currying the horses longer than necessary, while Grandma cooked this dish. Later, while the others enjoyed the pudding, he ate his supper of left-over peas and corn bread on the back steps, where he said the air was pure.

FIREPLACE RECIPE:

Chop 2 or 3 heads cabbage and boil. Pour off water, add new, then boil again. When tender, add beaten eggs, a little butter, a little thick sweet cream saved from the churn, and seasoning. Bake till done.

MODERN METHOD:

5	cups chopped cabbage	3 tablespoons half-and-half
3	eggs, beaten	$^1/_2$ teaspoon salt
2	tablespoons butter or margarine, melted	$^1/_8$ teaspoon black pepper

Place the cabbage in a saucepan, cover with water, and boil 10 minutes over high heat. Drain. Cover with water a second time and boil until tender. Drain and cool.

Preheat the oven to 350°. Add the eggs, butter, half-and-half, salt, and pepper to the cabbage. Pour into a buttered 2-quart casserole dish, and bake in the oven about 20 to 25 minutes, or until light brown. Serve hot with buttered corn bread. *Makes 6 servings*.

AUNT GUSSIE'S CORN OYSTERS

This is one of Aunt Gussie's prized concoctions. She declared that sometimes she couldn't cook and cool these delicacies fast enough to fill the little outstretched hands.

FIREPLACE RECIPE:

Scrape or grate a half-pint of tender fresh corn from the cob. Sift a little good flour and a few dashes of salt, and mix to a batter made with a beaten egg and a quarter pint of fresh sweet cream. Stir corn into the batter. Set fritter pan over medium hot coals, grease with a little butter, and drop mix by spoonfuls onto the pan. When one side is brown, turn and cook the other. Watch, as they scorch quickly. Serve warm or cold.

MODERN METHOD:

2 tablespoons flour	$^1/_2$ cup half-and-half
$^1/_2$ teaspoon baking powder	1 cup tender, fresh, grated corn
$^1/_2$ teaspoon salt	Butter or margarine for frying
1 egg, beaten	

Sift together the flour, baking powder, and salt. Blend in the egg and half-and-half, and add gradually to the flour mixture. Mix well. Add the corn.

Place a frying pan or griddle on medium heat, and grease it with a little butter. Drop the batter by spoonfuls into the hot pan. When one side is brown, turn and brown the other side, turning only once. Check often for scorching. Serve warm or cold. *Makes about 12 servings.*

ᴄᴏ AUNT CLARA'S CORN OMELET ᴄᴏ

*N*othing was wasted at Aunt Clara's house. When she shucked green corn, shucks went to the cows and cobs went to the hogs. Her eight- and ten-year-old daughters sewed the silks on their dolls' cotton-stuffed heads for hair—they plaited it, bunned it, or sometimes pompadoured it.

FIREPLACE RECIPE:

Shuck and clean silks from dozen or so ears of tender green corn. Boil. Split the kernels lengthwise of the ear with a sharp knife; then with a case knife scrape the corn from the cob.

Put to this half dozen eggs beaten so that whites and yolks are indistinguishable, and salt and pepper to suit the taste. Form into cakes, small or large as preferred, and fry to a golden brown, and you will have a very nice omelet.

MODERN METHOD:

12 ears fresh tender white corn	$^1/_2$ teaspoon pepper, or to taste
6 eggs, beaten well	Oil for griddle frying
1 teaspoon salt, or to taste	

Prepare the corn by removing the husks and silks. Fill a large container two-thirds full of water and bring to a full boil. Place the ears in the water and boil 3 to 5 minutes. Remove. Let cool. With a sharp knife, split each row of kernels. Splitting lengthwise allows the escape of the pulp while the hull is held on the cob. Remove any particles of hulls. With the back of a knife, scrape the pulp from the cob into a mixing bowl.

In another container, beat the eggs to one color and add the salt and pepper. Blend the egg mixture into the corn.

Spoon the batter into cakes about 4 inches in diameter, and fry on a greased griddle over medium heat until light brown, turning once. The cakes burn quickly if the griddle is very hot. Serve warm. *Makes 6 omelet cakes.*

⊷ SUNDAY HOMINY ⊶

*A*t the last corn harvest when the corn was dry, making lye hominy at Grandma's was a must. In the big black iron clothes-boiling pot, dried corn kernels were boiled in water mixed with wood ashes (lye), then rinsed in clear water time after time to wash away the lye. Then the corn was agitated with a paddle in water to remove the hulls and eyes and rinsed many more times. This was Grandma's favorite hominy dish.

FIREPLACE RECIPE:

Take a quart of lye hominy, mix with a little chopped onion and a finely chopped pickled chili pepper as to liking, and put in a mixing pan. Pour a pint jar half-full of fresh sweet milk, fill it to the top with sweet cream. Beat up 6 fresh-laid eggs and to this put a heavy spoon of salt, a dash or two of ground black pepper, the same of red pepper powder. Mix well the whole and pour into Dutch oven having a few spoonfuls of meat drippings. Cover and set on trivet over medium coals and bake.

Serve warm, either plain or with a bit of common white gravy.

MODERN METHOD:

$^1/_2$ cup milk	3 eggs, well beaten
$^1/_2$ cup half-and-half	$1^1/_2$ teaspoons salt
2 tablespoons butter or bacon drippings	$^1/_8$ teaspoon black pepper
2 cups hominy, drained (15-ounce can)	$^1/_8$ teaspoon red pepper
2 tablespoons onion, finely chopped	1 teaspoon chili powder

Preheat the oven to 350°. In a saucepan, heat the milk, half-and-half, and butter. Add the hominy and mix until smooth. Blend in onion, eggs, salt, peppers, and chili powder. Pour into a greased casserole. Bake uncovered in the oven 25 to 35 minutes or until firm and slightly brown on top. Test for firmness with a toothpick. Good plain or with thin White Gravy (see page 99). *Makes 6 servings.*

❧ PEASE PUDDING ❧

In cold wintertime, Grandma's family sat around the fire at suppertime eating hot Pease Pudding from bowls while they laughed and told hair-raising tales none of them really believed.

FIREPLACE RECIPE:

Soak a pound of dried split peas overnight in cold water. Come morning, drain and place in Dutch oven with a good size onion, a scrubbed turnip or two, several sticks of wild celery, 2 or 3 carrots if liked, all trimmed and chopped. Cover with water and place oven to boil, then remove hottest coals and simmer one hour. Take up, drain and run through sieve.

Put vegetables in bowl, add dollop of butter, a beaten egg, pepper, salt, tie in floured pudding cloth, drop in remaining liquid in Dutch oven. May need more. Place over coals and simmer 1 hour. Liquid is gravy.

MODERN METHOD:

1	cup dried split peas	1	egg, beaten
1	medium onion, sliced	2	tablespoons butter, melted
1	cup chopped celery	1	teaspoon flour
1	medium-size turnip, peeled and chopped		Salt and pepper
$^1/_2$	cup peeled and chopped carrots		

Cover the peas with water, plus 2 to 3 inches, and soak overnight. Drain the peas and place in a large saucepan. Barely cover with fresh water and cook until tendering begins. Remove from the heat and drain.

To the peas, add the onion, celery, turnip, and carrots. Cover with water. Bring to a boil, and immediately cut the heat down to simmer about 30 minutes or until all are very tender.

Preheat the oven to 325°. Drain the pea mixture in a colander, but save the broth. Run the mixture through a fine sieve. Add the egg, butter, and $^1/_4$ cup of the saved broth. Place the mixture in a greased casserole. Bake 20 to 25 minutes in the oven.

For gravy, blend the flour into the remaining broth, and cook until slightly thickened. Add the salt and pepper to taste. Pour into bowls for individual ladling. This dish is best when warmed over. *Makes 4 to 6 servings.*

∽ GREEN PEA STEW ∽

*W*hen Grandma wanted to make mayhaw jelly, Grandpa went to the creek to gather ripe mayhaws floating on the water that had fallen from the overhanging tree. She always had dry clothes and a pot of Green Pea Stew waiting. If he came up the lane swinging his bucket and whistling, she put away the Virginia snakeroot to heal moccasin bites and began warming the stew.

FIREPLACE RECIPE:

Wash and cut about a quarter pound of good salt meat into thin slices, cover with water in a stew pan and cook on trivet until almost done. To this put in bit of butter, a thin sliced onion, a quarter tea-cup tomato catsup, and a faggot* of parsley, and then a quart of good, fresh shelled field peas.

Simmer all over a slow fire till done and liquor is reduced. Take out the faggot and serve the rest together with corn dodger or spatter bread.

MODERN METHOD:

¹/₄ pound bacon	8 sprigs parsley tied with
1 tablespoon butter	string, loose end 10-inches long
¹/₄ cup diced onion	4 cups fresh shelled peas,
¹/₄ cup tomato catsup	black-eyed or field
	Salt

In a saucepan, cover the bacon with water and boil to half done. Stir in the butter, onion, and catsup. Add the parsley bundle, and tie the loose end of the string to the base of the pan handle. Then add the peas. Add just enough water to cover all. Simmer 25 to 35 minutes or until the peas are tender. Add a little water if needed. Salt to taste. Remove the parsley by the string and discard. Serve hot. Especially good with Spatter Bread and Chowchow (see pages 22 and 131). *Makes 8 servings.*

*A bundle tied together with thread or string.

POLE BEANS AND EGG DUMPLIN'S

*G*randma couldn't salvage many beans from the garden after the goats jumped the fence and ate their fill, then downed the stakes and tromped on the vines. She made the most of the bad luck with this succulent dish.

FIREPLACE RECIPE:

Take a bundle of 8 or 10 pole beans about the same length, washed and snipped, and corkscrew around same a thin piece of salt meat. Repeat to 8 bundles. Lay in spider pan, cover with water, raise to a boil, then simmer on low coals until beans are nice tender. Place on dish.

Pour pint of the broth in saucepan, add 4 or 5 spoonfuls of vinegar, a few pinches mustard. At full boil, put in 2 fresh-laid eggs beaten, fastly so as not to toughen, to cook separate as dumplings. Season, mix in crumbs of bread to thicken. Pour over the whole. Take to table hot.

MODERN METHOD:

1 to 1$^{1}/_{2}$ pounds pole (string) beans	$^{1}/_{4}$ teaspoon prepared mustard
$^{1}/_{2}$ pound smoked sliced bacon	Salt and pepper
2 cups broth from beans	2 eggs, beaten to one color
4 tablespoons cider vinegar	$^{3}/_{4}$ cup breadcrumbs, not too fine

Wash and snip the ends from the beans. Wrap bundles of eight beans barber-pole-style with a slice of bacon. Tuck under at the top. Lay the bundles in a heavy skillet with the ends of the bacon slices on the bottom of the pan. Cover with water and slow-simmer until the beans are tender. Transfer the beans from the pan into a deep dish, being careful to keep the bundles wrapped.

Pour the bean broth into a small saucepan. Add water as necessary to make 2 cups. Mix in the vinegar, mustard, and salt and pepper to taste. Bring to a hard boil, and drop in a spoonful of the eggs one at a time, as quickly as possible, to cook separately as dumplings. Prolonged cooking toughens the eggs. Remove from the heat.

Lightly mix in the breadcrumbs, leaving some lumps, and pour the mixture over the bean bundles in the dish. Serve hot. *Makes 8 servings.*

VARIATIONS: Stir in $^{1}/_{4}$ cup grated cheese or $^{1}/_{4}$ cup coarsely chopped Parched (Toasted) Pecans (see page 190) before serving.

⧼ NUTTY POTATO LOAF ⧽

*G*randma used potatoes, especially grated, to soothe and heal sunburn, cure warts and other ailments, as well as to cook for food. This nutty loaf was often on the table when ripe peanuts were pulled from the ground, dried, and roasted in the Dutch oven in the fireplace.

FIREPLACE RECIPE:

Put a little chopped celery with a few leaves and a handful of well-scrubbed potato peelings in a stew pan with a little salted water. Boil over fire till tender and pour away water. To this put 1½ pints of cooked, mashed Irish potatoes, not too dry. Now beat in two frothed eggs, butter as desired, and a small sweet onion grated.

Tie ½ pint of freshly parched and shelled peanuts in a muslin cloth and beat to small pieces, sprinkle with a little salt, then add to mix. Bake in Dutch oven with a few sheets of paper in the bottom till done.

MODERN METHOD:

3 cups mashed potatoes, about 1½ pounds raw	½ cup water
½ plus ¼ teaspoon salt	2 eggs, beaten
½ cup chopped celery	2 tablespoons butter or margarine, melted
1 tablespoon chopped celery leaves	2 tablespoons sweet onion, grated
¼ cup cooked, chopped potato peelings, about ½ cup uncooked	¾ cup crunchy peanut butter

Wash, scrub, and peel the potatoes; save the peelings. Cube the potatoes. Place in a large pot, cover with water, add the ½ teaspoon salt, and cook until tender. Drain and mash.

In another pot, mix the celery and leaves, potato peelings, and the remaining ¼ teaspoon salt. Cover with the ½ cup water and simmer until slightly tender. Drain, mash to lumpy with a fork, add to the mashed potatoes, and mix. Blend in the eggs, butter, onion, and peanut butter.

Preheat the oven to 350°. Place the potato mixture in a greased 9 x 5-inch loaf pan, pack down firmly with the back of a spoon, and bake in the oven 30 minutes or until a toothpick inserted in the center comes out clean. Slice and serve cold or reheated. *Makes 8 servings.*

⚜ SQUASH MUFFINS ⚜

*B*efore Aunt Daisy learned to heavily grease the muffin pans, muffins stuck so tight she claimed they reminded her of the time the preacher baptized her in the creek. When he pulled her up out of the water, her clothes clung to her body tight as those muffins were glued to the pan. Said she felt like a plucked chicken and knew she looked like one.

FIREPLACE RECIPE:

Mix a pound of sugar with adequate butter and eggs as for cake. Put to this about 3 tea-cups of good flour mixed with adequate baking powder and salt.

Add not quite half as much squash as flour, about a pint, handful of pecans, and wet all with rich milk to a nice dough.

Bake in muffin pan in Dutch oven on fairly hot coals until brown. While hot, put melted butter and sugar sprinklings on tops.

MODERN METHOD:

$^{1}/_{3}$ cup butter or margarine	$1^{1}/_{2}$ cups acorn, butternut, or
1 cup sugar	other squash, cooked and mashed
3 eggs, beaten	$^{1}/_{4}$ cup finely chopped pecans
$1^{3}/_{4}$ cups all-purpose flour	Melted butter or margarine to brush tops
2 teaspoons baking powder	Sugar to sprinkle tops
$^{1}/_{4}$ teaspoon salt	
$^{2}/_{3}$ cup half-and-half	

Preheat the oven to 400°. Cream the butter and sugar. Add the beaten eggs. Sift together the flour, baking powder, and salt, and add to the butter mixture alternately with the half-and-half. Blend in the squash and pecans.

Place baking cups in a 12-cup muffin pan, fill two-thirds full with the squash, and bake 20 to 25 minutes or until slightly brown. Remove from the pan. Brush the tops with melted butter and sprinkle with sugar. *Makes 1 dozen muffins.*

GRANDMA'S SWEET POTATO PONE

*R*abbits loved Grandma's tender sweet potato vines. When she found them eaten down to the ground, she used scare tactics by placing empty canning jars inside the garden fence on the woodsy side. Even a slight breeze blowing over the tops of the jars sent out enough ghostly murmurs to keep the rabbits away.

FIREPLACE METHOD:

Choose unblemished sweet potatoes, four. Wash and brush very clean and run over fine grater. In mixing pan put 2 fresh-laid eggs and whip to one color. To this add a quarter-pint good molasses and a walnut-size lump of butter which melt.

Put to the whole the same amount of cornmeal as molasses to which has been thrown in proper salt and to this put family's desires of spices. Blend all properly and shape into a pone and bake slow in Dutch oven with a few coals in lid until done. Good with a dish of pork, any kind.

MODERN METHOD:

4   cups grated, raw, unpeeled sweet potatoes
3   eggs, well beaten
3/4 cup sugarcane molasses
2   tablespoons butter or margarine, melted

3/4 cup cornmeal
1   teaspoon baking powder
1/2 teaspoon salt
    Spices as desired

Preheat the oven to 375°. Scrub the potatoes clean and grate finely in a mixing bowl. Add the eggs, molasses, and butter. Combine the cornmeal, baking powder, salt, and spices, and thoroughly blend into the potato and egg mixture.

Shape into a loaf resembling French bread, and place on a lightly greased cookie sheet. Bake in the oven for 35 to 45 minutes or until brown and a thin knife blade inserted in the center comes out clean. Remove. Cool and slice. Best served with pork. Also makes a tasty snack sliced, buttered, and toasted. *Makes 8 to 10 servings.*

⤞ TURNIP SOUP ⤝

*A*unt Carrie Lambert gave Grandma her recipe for this soup. It had no meat stock, only turnip boilings. Grandma said it was the nearest thing to water she'd ever tasted, and added goodies to make it delicious.

FIREPLACE RECIPE:

Fry 2 thin slices ham in spider on trivet over hot coals. Take up and let wait. In ham drippings, melt 2 tablespoons butter, add 4 medium size unpeeled turnips thinly sliced, and 1 medium size onion sliced thin. Add a cup of fresh rain water, cover, and slow cook till all is tender. Add 4 cups beef or other stock, cover, and simmer 20 to 25 minutes. Rub through sieve. If desired, chop ham into bits and add. Re-heat and serve hot.

MODERN METHOD:

2	thin slices smoked ham	1	onion, size of an egg
2	tablespoons butter or margarine	4	cups beef stock
4	medium-size turnips, unpeeled, and thinly sliced		

Combine the ham, butter, turnips, onion, and beef stock in a saucepan over medium heat. Slow-simmer the mixture until all is tender, and then rub it through a sieve. Serve hot. *Makes 6 servings.*

IMPOTENCY

Take of ants, 1 lb.; boiling water 4 lbs. Infuse for three hours, press out the liquor, and strain. This is an excellent stimulant, and is used as a lotion in impotency.

—From *Mackenzie's Five Thousand Receipts* (1852)

⤳ TURNIP HASH ⤳

*G*randma usually served this supper dish with hot, crunchy Corn Fritters topped with melted butter and a bowl of Aunt Sally's Hot Pot (see page 52), a variation of chili.

FIREPLACE RECIPE:

Peel a few turnips and dice for a pint. Put to this, tender kernels of 2 or 3 roasting ears and cover all with salted water. Place in Dutch oven on trivet in a mound of boiling-coals and cook. Drain. Fry a sweet onion and a few sprigs of parsley in a walnut-size dollop of butter and put to turnips with a few dashes ground black pepper, and a little cream. Let the whole boil up once, then simmer down and take away.

Corn fritters: mix 3 or 4 egg yolks, dollop of butter. Add milk to $\frac{1}{2}$ pint cornmeal, a little flour, salt, whipped egg whites. Fry on hot griddle.

MODERN METHOD:

2 cups unpeeled, diced turnip roots	$^3/_4$ cup onions rings
2 cups tender whole kernel corn	2 tablespoons finely chopped parsley
$^3/_4$ teaspoon salt	$^1/_4$ teaspoon black pepper
$^1/_2$ cup half-and-half	$^1/_2$ cup cheddar cheese, grated
2 level tablespoons butter or margarine	Corn Fritters (optional, recipe follows)

Place the turnips, corn, and salt in a saucepan and barely cover with water. Boil slowly until tender. Drain. Add the half-and-half.

Place the butter in a frying pan, and sauté the onions with the parsley. Add the turnips. With a lid partially on, slow-simmer the mixture 10 to15 minutes, or until little liquid remains. Remove from the heat, drain, and mash one-fourth of the vegetables, leaving the balance in chunks. Spoon into a serving dish and sprinkle with the black pepper. Top with the grated cheese. Serve with Corn Fritters, if desired. *Makes about 2 cups.*

Corn Fritters

2 egg yolks, well beaten
1 tablespoon butter or margarine, melted
3/4 teaspoon salt
1 cup cornmeal
1 cup milk
2 egg whites, stiffly beaten
1/4 cup all-purpose flour
2 tablespoons oil for griddle

Mix the egg yolks, butter, salt, and cornmeal. Add the milk. Fold in the egg whites and flour. Batter must be thin. Place 2 spoonfuls at a time on a hot, oiled griddle. Brown each side. *Makes about 8 fritters*.

CEMENT FOR GLUEING CHINA OR GLASS

A cheap cement is made by burning oyster-shells and pulverizing the lime from them very fine; then mixing it with white of egg to a thick paste and applying it to the china or glass, and securing the pieces together until dry.

When it is dry, it takes a very long soaking to become soft again. I have lifted thirty pounds by the stem of a wine glass, which had been broken and mended with this cement. Common lime will do but it is not so good; either should be freshly burned, and only mix what is needed, for when once dry, you cannot soften it.

—From *Dr. Chase's Recipes* (1867)

CARRIE MAE'S SASSY TURNIPS

When cousin Carrie Mae came up with this turnip dish, she said she could remember being that tickled only one other time. That was the day she learned to shoot old Bossy's milk directly into the bucket instead of on her own shoes.

FIREPLACE RECIPE:

Wash, scrape turnips, cut in small pieces. Put in proper salt and sugar. Add water, put all in kettle and hang over slow fire. Cook till tender. Drain and dry. Roll in egg and flour. Put butter in spider on medium hot coals and fry turnips brown. Drain fat, add a little vinegar, pepper, lemon juice. Make white sauce and while hot, add a little clabber cheese and mix all well together with turnips. Serve with fresh-corn spoon bread.

MODERN METHOD:

4 cups turnips, about $1^1/_2$ pounds raw	4 tablespoons butter or margarine
1 teaspoon salt	1 tablespoon vinegar
$^1/_4$ teaspoon sugar	2 tablespoons lemon juice
1 egg, well beaten	$^1/_8$ teaspoon black pepper
Flour for dredging	Cheese Sauce (recipe follows)

Wash and scrape the turnips. Cut into $^1/_2$-inch cubes. Place in a saucepan with water to cover. Add the salt and sugar. Cover and cook over low heat 12 to 15 minutes or until tender but still crunchy. Discard the liquid. Drain on a paper towel. When dry, dredge the cubes in the beaten egg, then the flour; repeat the procedure.

Place the butter in a frying pan over medium heat. Fry the turnips to a brown coat. Drain the fat. Add the vinegar, lemon juice, and black pepper. Mix well, simmer 4 or 5 minutes, and remove from the heat. Take up on a platter and top with Cheese Sauce. Good with Roasting-Ear Spoon Bread (see page 24). *Makes 8 servings.*

Cheese Sauce

1   tablespoon each flour and cornstarch 1   cup fat-free milk
2   tablespoons cooking oil $^1/_2$ cup grated cheddar cheese

Mix the flour and cornstarch into the cooking oil. Add the milk gradually, stir until smooth, and cook over low heat or in a double boiler over hot water, stirring constantly until thickened. Stir in the cheese and beat until well blended. *Makes about 1 cup.*

TO PROCURE SLEEP

Pour a pint of boiling water on an ounce of Epsom salts. Set it to cool and drink it on going to bed. If still disturbed, count from 1 to 1000. Sleep will generally come on before the person has reached 500.

Or, on going to bed, take a warm bath.

Or, rub the body well with rough towels or with the flesh-brush for a quarter of an hour.

If this does not procure sound sleep, take a tea-spoon of magnesia in a wine glass of water, with or without a few drops of hartshorn.

—From *Mackenzie's Five Thousand Receipts* (1852)

TURNIP GREENS AND CORN DUMPLIN'S WITH OKRA STICKS

*G*randma always said her okra gathering served a dual purpose. She used the pods for succulent dishes and picked extra leaves to crumple and place on cuts; the broken veins in the leaves let out the antiseptic.

FIREPLACE RECIPE:

In kettle over fire, fry small slab of salt meat. Add turnip greens with stems removed and in faggot*, and water to cover. Swing covered kettle over slow fire. Boil till almost done. Remove faggot.

Make dumplings with a pint of cornmeal, dash of flour, a little salt, some soda, a measure of baking powder, a tad of vinegar, a little horseradish root scraped and grated. To this put buttermilk for a thick dough, then mix in a frothed egg. Roll tight into balls smaller than walnuts and drop on greens, not in liquor. Cook till done. Garnish with dumplings.

Have ready 2 or 3 handfuls of okra pods washed, trimmed, and sliced lengthwise. Soak a few minutes in frothed egg. Roll in seasoned cornmeal and fry brittle in spider in sizzling lard. Serve with turnips and dumplings.

MODERN METHOD:

Turnip Greens

6   slices bacon, coarsely chopped
1   large bunch turnip greens, about 12 cups, cleaned and torn into pieces

Place the bacon in a large kettle, and fry over medium heat until almost done but not brown. Add the greens, devoid of long stems, and cover with water. (Large stems may be tied with thread and boiled with greens for strength and vitamins.) Cook covered over simmering heat 15 to 20 minutes, depending on the age of the greens, or until almost tender. Remove the bunch of stems. Add the dumplings.

*A bundle tied together with thread or string.

80

Dumplings and Assembly

2 cups cornmeal	$^3/_4$ cup buttermilk
$^1/_4$ cup all-purpose flour	2 teaspoons prepared horseradish
$1^1/_2$ teaspoons baking powder	1 egg, beaten
$^1/_2$ teaspoon baking soda	1 tablespoon vinegar
1 teaspoon salt	

Sift together the cornmeal, flour, baking powder, baking soda, and salt. Blend in the buttermilk a little at a time. Mix the horseradish and egg, and stir into the dough. Add the vinegar. Dough should be stiff.

Flour your hands and roll the dough into small, tight balls. Lay the dough balls gently on top of the greens to steam. Remove a little of the liquid if necessary. Cover and cook over medium-slow heat 15 to 18 minutes. Remove the dumplings gently. Set aside and keep warm.

Chop the greens and place on a platter. Add 2 or 3 spoonfuls of juice if dry. Place the dumplings around the edge of the dish. Serve hot. *Makes 8 servings*.

Okra Sticks

10 small tender okra pods, washed, stemmed, and halved lengthwise	$^1/_2$ cup cornmeal mixed with
	$^1/_4$ teaspoon salt and dash of pepper
	Oil to fry
1 egg, beaten frothy	

Cook the okra sticks while the dumplings are cooking. Soak the sticks in the egg at least 10 minutes; remove, being careful not to let the egg drain off. Quickly roll in the cornmeal. Fry in hot oil until brown and crisp. Remove and drain on a paper towel. Serve as a side dish with the greens. *Makes 8 servings*.

AUNT HATTIE MAE'S ONION PIE IN CRACKLIN' PASTRY

*A*unt Hattie loved serving this pie often with the traditional New Year's Day dish of a big bowl of juicy black-eyed peas simmered all morning with ham hock.

FIREPLACE RECIPE:

For pastry, take a pint of flour mixed with little cornmeal, put in $1/4$ pint fresh, fried-meat grease and handful of mashed brittle bacon, and make stiff dough. Divide in two parts; roll one out, lay in bottom of pan. Bake a few minutes to set. Roll other dough to lay over filling.

Take 4 or 5 sweet onions, peeled, sliced, fry in spider in lard till done. Discard lard. Mix in 2-3 eggs, a little flour, $1/2$ pint rich milk, salt, pepper. Pour into pastry pan. Add top, bake. Top with bacon crumbles.

MODERN METHOD:

Double Crust Cracklin' Pastry

10 slices bacon	$1/2$ cup bacon drippings
$1^3/4$ cups flour	3 to 4 tablespoons cold water
$1/4$ cup cornmeal	$1/4$ cup bacon as above, crumbled

Fry the bacon crisply and crumble finely. Set aside 2 tablespoons for topping the pastry. Save the drippings.

Preheat the oven to 425°. Sift the flour and cornmeal together and work in the bacon drippings. The mixture will be grainy. Sprinkle with the water to make a stiff dough. If too dry, add a little cooking oil. Mix the crumbled bacon in with the flour mixture. Squeeze the dough to a tight ball, and then divide it in half. Save one half for the top crust.

Place one half the dough between two pieces of waxed paper, and roll to $1/4$-inch thickness, a little larger than the pie pan. Peel the paper from the top of the dough, invert the dough into the pan, and fit it in carefully. Remove the remaining paper and discard. Bake the crust 10 minutes in the oven until lightly browned. Remove and cool.

Filling and Assembly

3 cups sweet onions, preferably white, peeled and thinly sliced

3 tablespoons shortening or oil for frying

2 tablespoons flour

Salt and pepper

2 eggs, beaten

1 cup half-and-half

Cook the onions in the oil over very low heat until transparent but not brown. Remove. Drain and discard the fat.

Preheat the oven to 325°. In a mixing bowl, sift the flour together with the salt and pepper to taste. Blend the eggs and half-and-half, and add this to the flour mix. Stir in the onions, being careful not to mush them. Pour into the readied crust.

Roll the remaining dough between waxed paper as before. Place over the filling, crimp under the bottom crust with wet fingers, and prick the top crust with a fork. Brush lightly with milk for even browning. Bake in the oven 25 to 30 minutes or until brown. Garnish the top with the 2 tablespoons reserved crushed bacon. Serve hot. *Makes 6 servings.*

PARSLEY

The uses of parsley, in cookery, both for sauce and garnish, are numerous and well known. It is however, poisonous to several kinds of birds; and although so commonly used at the table, facts have been adduced from which it would appear that, in some constitutions, it occasions epilepsy, or at least aggravates the fits in those who are subject to that disease. Inflamation in the eyes has also been attributed to the use of it.

Both the roots and seed are employed in medicine.

—From *Useful Knowledge* by Reverend William Bingley (1818)

❧ AUNT GUSSIE'S CABBAGE PIE ❧

*G*randma said that unlike Aunt Hattie Mae, who got a kick out of broadcasting her recipes to show off her cooking expertise, Aunt Gussie kept her favorite recipes to herself. She accidentally let this one slip out trying to out-brag Aunt Hattie.

FIREPLACE RECIPE:

Put a hickory nut-size lump of lard in a spider pan over slow coals, melt. Put to it a small head of cabbage chopped for overly full quart. Cook and stir till almost done, not brown. To this put a little milk and ½ pint finely shredded hoop cheese. Stir till melted over.

Now put in onion cut fine, dash of salt, of black pepper, of red. Stir well. Pour all into Dutch oven oiled on bottom and sides; coat with dry cornmeal. Over this pour a thin batter of cornmeal, flour, rising, egg, milk, butter, and sprinkle a spoon of dry meal on top. Bake like bread.

MODERN METHOD:

3 tablespoons vegetable oil	Salt and black pepper
6 cups shredded cabbage, about 1½ pounds	1 cup shredded cheddar cheese
½ cup milk	Dry cornmeal for sprinkling
1 teaspoon chopped onion	Cornmeal Topping (recipe follows)
¼ teaspoon red pepper	

Place the oil in a large frying pan, add the cabbage, and cook on lowest heat, stirring constantly until the cabbage is slightly tender, 12 to 15 minutes. Do not scorch. Add the milk and mix thoroughly. Add the onion, red pepper, salt and black pepper to taste, and mix well. Blend in the cheese.

Preheat the oven to 425°. Grease the bottom and sides of a 2-quart casserole, and sprinkle lightly with the dry cornmeal. Pour in the cabbage mix and level the mixture. With a knife make several thin pockets on the sides of the filling for the Cornmeal Topping to run into. Pour the Cornmeal Topping over the filling. Sprinkle a spoon of the dry meal on top. Bake for 15 to 20 minutes or until the top is nicely browned. Serve hot. *Makes 6 servings.*

Cornmeal Topping

3/4 cup cornmeal mixed
    with 1/4 cup flour
2 teaspoons baking powder
1/2 teaspoon salt

3/4 cup milk
1 egg, well beaten
2 tablespoons butter or margarine, melted

Sift together the cornmeal/flour mix, baking powder, and salt. Mix the milk, egg, and butter together and add slowly to the dry mix. Blend well.

TO PRODUCE A FAC-SIMILE OF ANY WRITING

The pen should be made of glass enamel; the point being small and finely polished; so that the part above the point may be large enough to hold as much ink as, or more than a common writing pen.

A mixture of equal parts of Frankfort black, and fresh butter, is now to be smeared over sheets of paper, and rubbed off after a certain time. The paper, thus smeared, is to be pressed for some hours; taking care to have sheets of blotting-paper between each of the sheets of black paper.

When fit for use, writing paper is put between sheets of blackened paper, and the upper sheet is to be written on, with common writing ink, by the glass or enamel pen.

By this method, not only the copy is obtained on which the pen writes, but also, two, or more, made by means of the blackened paper.

—From *Mackenzie's Five Thousand Receipts* (1852)

COUSIN LILLIE MAE'S TOMATO PIE IN POTATO CRUST

*C*ousin Lillie Mae had three un-pretty daughters she tried hard for years to marry off. She finally caught a husband for the thirty-year-old with this pie.

FIREPLACE RECIPE:

Make crust as thus: Boil Irish potatoes, salt, mash smooth. Mix to this a fresh egg, a few parsley sprigs cut fine. Pat mix into pie pan, shape ready for filling.

Then take a half-dozen ripe tomatoes and cut into thick slices. Coat with salted and peppered flour and fry in spider pan in hot meat grease till brown. Take up into bowl, add a little fresh sweet cream, sprinkle some bread crumbs, a few dill leaves cut fine, and spoon onto potato crust. Set in pan in Dutch oven and bake until brown. Spread a little shredded hoop cheese on top before taking to table.

MODERN METHOD:

Potato Crust

3	cups mashed potatoes, about 6 medium potatoes	1	egg, beaten
$^1/_2$	teaspoon salt	2	tablespoons finely chopped parsley

Cover the potatoes with water, cook until tender, drain, and mash. Add the salt. When cool, blend in the egg and parsley. Carefully pat the mix to a thickness of $^1/_2$ to $^3/_4$ inches in the bottom and on the sides of a 9-inch pie pan.

Filling and Assembly

6	large ripe tomatoes, sliced $^1/_4$ inch thick	$^1/_2$	cup bacon grease for frying, or butter or margarine
$^1/_2$	cup all-purpose flour for dredging	1	tablespoon fresh dill leaves, finely chopped
$^1/_2$	teaspoon salt	$^1/_4$	cup cream or half-and-half
$^1/_2$	teaspoon black pepper	$^1/_2$	cup stale breadcrumbs
		$^1/_2$	cup shredded cheddar cheese

Dredge the tomato slices in a mix of flour, salt, and pepper. Place the bacon grease or butter in a large frying pan, and slow-fry the tomato slices until brown but not quite done, turning once. Add the dill leaves to the cream, and pour over the tomatoes in the pan. Mix in the breadcrumbs, and stir gently with a fork, being careful not to crush the tomatoes.

Preheat the oven to 400°. Remove the tomatoes from the heat and carefully spoon them into the potato pastry. Level the mixture. Bake in the oven for 20 to 25 minutes, or until golden brown. Remove from the oven. Sprinkle the top with cheese, more if needed, and let stand a few minutes. Serve hot in the casserole or spoon into a dish. Good accompaniment for vegetables or meats. *Makes 6 to 8 servings.*

DRESSING FOR FIREPLACE COOKING

While cooking at the fireplace, it was necessary to wear proper clothing. Ankle-length aprons with long bibs that went around the neck and sashes that tied at the back, kept full skirts pulled close to the body. A long-billed bonnet temporarily eliminated heat from the face by a nod. Extreme care had to be taken to avoid burns to hands and arms. Iron pots stay hot a long time, and when it was necessary to handle them after being removed from the fire with pot hooks, very thick cotton-quilted potholders were mandatory.

⚮ AUNT ELLA'S ⚮
GREEN TOMATO PIE

*A*unt Ella always had tomatoes before anyone else in the area. She planted early and covered the tender plants with pine tree bark during pre-spring freezes. She let her pie do her bragging at the church's All-Day Singing and Dinner on the Ground. But Grandma said she always mouthed a little help for it.

FIREPLACE RECIPE:

Slice thin a half dozen green tomatoes, put in pan, and cover with water. Add few lemon slices. Cook tomatoes till done, not wilty. Cool, add crumb of a biscuit, dash of flour, a little sugar, pinch of salt. Cook till a little thick. Mix in a lump of butter, pour into pan lined with pastry and cover with same. Bake in Dutch oven over hot coals, a few coals in lid.

MODERN METHOD:

Pastry

$2^1/4$ cups flour	$3/4$ cup shortening
$1/2$ teaspoon baking powder	4 to 6 tablespoons cold water
1 teaspoon salt	

First make a double-crust, 9-inch pastry shell. In a bowl, sift together the flour, baking powder, and salt. Cut in the shortening to pea size. Gradually add the water to make a stiff dough. Divide the dough into two parts, one slightly larger than the other. Roll out the larger on a floured board to $1/8$-inch thickness, and place it firmly in the pie tin. Roll out the other portion for the top crust.

Filling and Assembly

3 cups green tomatoes, cut into thick slices	1 cup sugar
1 tablespoon water	$1/4$ teaspoon salt
$1/3$ lemon, thinly sliced	$1/4$ cup salty cracker crumbs
1 tablespoon flour	3 tablespoons butter, melted
	1 tablespoon milk for brushing pastry

Preheat the oven to 375°. Place the tomatoes, water, and lemon in a saucepan. Cover and simmer 8 to 10 minutes until the tomatoes are slightly limp. Remove them from the heat and cool. There should be a little juice. Blend the flour, sugar, and salt into the tomatoes. Return the saucepan to the heat and cook until a little thick.

In a cup, stir the cracker crumbs into the butter and add to the mixture. Pour into the pie shell, and cover with the top sheet of dough. Pinch the sides to seal, brush the top lightly with milk, and prick the top crust with a fork. Bake in the oven 25 to 30 minutes or until brown. *Makes 6 servings.*

TOAD OINTMENT

For sprains, strains, lame-back, rheumatism, caked breasts, caked udders, &c., &c. Good sized live toads, 4 in number; put into boiling water and cook very soft; then take them out and boil the water down to $\frac{1}{2}$ pt., and add fresh churned unsalted butter 1 lb. and simmer together; at the last add tincture of arnica* 2 ozs.

This was obtained from an old Physician, who thought more of it than of any other prescription in his possession. Some persons might think it hard on toads, but you could not kill them quicker in any other way.

—From *Dr. Chase's Recipes* (1867)

*Tincture of dried arnica flower heads.

⌒ ASPARAGUS PIE ⌒

*G*randpa heard that asparagus was grown in shallow, stagnant minnow ponds—thus accounting for the green color. Said it was too polluted to even taste. The rest of the family thought it was delicious.

FIREPLACE RECIPE:

Boil 2 or 3 handfuls asparagus tips and set aside. Mix several beaten eggs with some minced boiled ham, put in a little milk and some flour for thickening. Cook till thick as wanted. Add seasoning. Pour into pastry crust and cover with top crust. Bake till brown.

MODERN METHOD:

1 recipe Flaky Paste (see page 157)	1 tablespoon butter or margarine, melted
2 tablespoons flour	Salt and pepper
1 tablespoon cornstarch	$^1/_2$ cup finely minced boiled ham
4 eggs, beaten to an even color	$2^1/_2$ cups asparagus tips and
1 cup plus 1 tablespoon milk	chopped tender stems, cooked

Preheat the oven to 450°. Prepare the pastry for a standard, 9-inch, double-crust pie, using the Flaky Paste recipe. Roll out and fit the bottom crust in a pie plate. Prick the bottom three or four times with a fork, and bake in the oven 5 to 7 minutes until partially done. Remove the crust and reduce the oven temperature to 400°. Roll out the top crust to have ready.

Mix the flour and cornstarch in the top of a double boiler. Blend the eggs with 1 cup milk, and slowly spoon the egg mixture into the flour mixture. Beat until smooth. Add the butter, salt and pepper to taste (remember that the ham is salty), and the ham. Place the top of the double boiler over simmering water, and cook, stirring constantly, until the mixture coats a spoon. Remove from the heat. Carefully fold in the asparagus and pour the mixture into the pastry crust. Cover with the top crust, thinly paint it with the remaining 1 tablespoon milk, and bake in the oven 8 to 10 minutes until the top is golden brown. *Makes 6 servings.*

Gravies,
Sauces, and
Syrups

❧ RED-EYE GRAVY ❧

*G*randpa had a flat tire while plowing in the field with the Model T. After patching the tube with the patch kit and inserting a boot in the tire, he pumped it up, then angrily parked the car in the barn. Grandma said she calmed his frustration with eggs and ham in a pool of his favorite Red-Eye Gravy. And, of course, a mound of grits on the side.

FIREPLACE RECIPE:

Lay a good size cured, hickory-smoked ham slice in spider and fry over medium hot coals till both sides are very brown. Take up, pour in a little hot water. Scrape ham leavings from sides and bottom and give it a boil.

MODERN METHOD:

1 tablespoon butter or margarine

$^1/_2$ to $^3/_4$ pound hickory-smoked ham slice, about $^1/_2$ inch thick

$^1/_2$ to $^2/_3$ cup cold water

Melt the butter in a frying pan, and add the ham (cook in a heavy, black iron frying pan for best flavor). Cook slowly, turning often to brown both sides. Do not burn. The brown makes the gravy rich and tasty.

Remove the ham from the pan. Scrape all the particles from the sides and bottom of the pan, and add the water to the pan to make the gravy. Simmer-cook a few minutes over low heat until the gravy is a dark reddish brown and tasty. Serve hot. *Makes about 1 cup.*

NOTE: Similar gravy can be made by adding a few tablespoons of black coffee to bacon drippings. However, this is not the true red-eye and does not have the deep, rich flavor. Genuine Red-Eye Gravy has no coffee.

❦ HORSERADISH GRAVY ❧

*C*ousin Willie Mae bragged about being a genius at cooking and gave Grandma this recipe. Grandma made it, but nobody would eat it until she upgraded it. Grandma said Willie Mae's cooking was in the incubation stage.

FIREPLACE RECIPE:

Put some meat stock in a pan over slack heat. Mix in a little flour for thickening, stir smooth, and boil lightly till thick as wanted. Take from heat and add some horse-radish, a pinch each of sugar and salt.

MODERN METHOD:

2	cups meat stock	$1/4$	teaspoon sugar
1	tablespoon flour	$1/8$	teaspoon salt
4	tablespoons horseradish root, grated		

Mix together the stock, flour, horseradish, sugar, and salt. Bring to a low boil over medium heat and cook until slightly thick. Serve hot. *Makes 2 cups.*

HORSE-RADISH

The root of horse-radish is much used for culinary purposes. It is remarkable for great pungency both of smell and taste. When scraped, it is mixed with pickles to heighten their flavor, and is eaten with roast-beef, fish, and several other kinds of food.

Horse-radish is also in considerable repute as a medicine, and is a powerful stimulant, whether externally or internally applied. Notwithstanding this we are informed by Dr. Withering that an infusion of horse-radish in cold milk is one of the best and safest cosmetics* known.

—From *Useful Knowledge* by Reverend William Bingley (1818)

*Treatments serving to beautify the body.

❧ STRAWBERRY GRAVY ❧

*G*randma made the plainest of food taste elegant with her succulent Strawberry Gravy.

FIREPLACE RECIPE:

To make strawberry gravy, lay a little smokehouse side meat sliced in spider pan, fry brittle, and put to wait.

Boil sugar with a little flour and enough water for thin syrup in saucepan in Dutch oven with a little water in bottom. Put in double handful red ripe strawberries mashed good. Simmer until done and put in a spoon or two of bottom meat grease.

MODERN METHOD:

$1/2$	pound smoked bacon	1	cup water
1	tablespoon flour	$1^1/2$	cups ripe strawberries, puréed*
1	cup sugar		

Place the bacon in a cold skillet. Cook over moderate heat, turning frequently. Remove the bacon from the pan when crisp. Drain on a paper towel, and set aside to serve with the gravy or for other use. Discard the grease, but save 1 tablespoon of the drippings (dregs) in the skillet for use later.

In a saucepan, combine the flour with the sugar, and add the water a little at a time. Beat until smooth. Place the mixture over low heat, and boil to a thin syrup, stirring often. Add the mashed or puréed berries. Simmer until the berries are well cooked and pour the berry mixture into the skillet with the drippings. Simmer 3 minutes and remove from the heat. Serve warm with Fried Biscuits (see page 29) or other biscuits. *Makes about 1 1/2 cups.*

*A 10-ounce package of frozen, sliced, and sweetened strawberries may be substituted for sugar, water, and berries. Taste the gravy for the desired sweetness.

⤬ COCOA GRAVY ⤬

*G*randma concocted this recipe especially to see the grandchildren's smiles when they came to the table.

FIREPLACE RECIPE:

Take a tea-cup of cocoa powder and the same of sugar and mix with a little flour.
Dribble in a tea-cup of thin cream mixed with a little water. Put all together in a pan
over a finger of boiling water in Dutch oven. Stir till cooks to gravy, put in a lump of
butter and mix. Serve over fried or regular biscuits.

MODERN METHOD:

1	cup cocoa powder	1	tablespoon cornstarch
1 1/2	cups sugar	1	cup half-and-half
1/2	teaspoon salt	1/4	cup water
1	teaspoon flour	2	tablespoons butter or margarine

In the top of a double boiler, mix the cocoa, sugar, salt, flour, and cornstarch. Blend in the
cream and water and cook over boiling water, stirring constantly. Cook until the mixture
slightly coats the back of the spoon and remove from the heat. Add the butter and mix thoroughly. Serve warm over Fried Biscuits or Flapjacks (see pages 29 and 40). *Makes about 1 1/2 cups.*

HAIR LOTION

One pint of rosewater, one ounce of cologne, one half ounce of
vinegar of cantharides*. The scalp should be brushed briskly
until red and the lotion applied daily..

—From *The Housekeeper Cook Book* (1894)

*A toxic preparation of the crushed, dried, bodies of beetles

---

ORANGE GRAVY

*G*randma said she got this from her do-good grandmother who fed her heart by keeping others straight. Called it a refreshing gravy for bread dressings and meats. This has been a second gravy in our family for cornbread dressing at Thanksgiving, the first being giblet gravy.

FIREPLACE RECIPE:

Put some thinly sliced onion in stew pan with meat stock, some juice of a sweet orange along with coarsely chopped orange peel, and a little lemon peel, sugar to taste, and low-simmer till tender. Do not boil.

MODERN METHOD:

$^1/_4$ cup thinly sliced onion

$1^1/_2$ cups meat stock

$^1/_4$ cup juice of a sweet orange

$^1/_2$ cup coarsely chopped orange peel

2   tablespoons chopped lemon peel

$^1/_2$ to 1 teaspoon sugar, or to taste

1   tablespoon flour

Put the sliced onion in a stew pot with the meat stock, orange juice, orange peel, lemon peel, and sugar. Low-simmer for 15 to 20 minutes until the peels are tender. Do not boil.

Remove from the heat and let cool. Blend in the flour, return the mixture to the stove, and continue to cook over low heat until slightly thickened. If not tart enough, simmer a little longer. Serve strained or unstrained. Take to the table hot. *Makes about 1½ cups.*

❧ HONEY GRAVY ❧

*T*here was plenty of fresh honey at Grandma's when bee-hives were robbed. She added honey to most foods whether they needed sweetening or not, saying honey was concentrated nectar from health-giving herbs.

FIREPLACE RECIPE:

Beat up yolk of egg. Pour in of honey, 4 long foot pats. To this add several pinches of flour, a short tea-cup of fresh, thin sweet cream and a few tricklings of juice of lemon. Set pan over boiling water in Dutch oven and cook until slightly thickened. Good on fried biscuits and meats.

MODERN METHOD:

1 cup half-and-half, less 1 tablespoon	1 tablespoon flour
1 egg yolk, well beaten	2 tablespoons lemon juice
1/3 cup honey	

In the top of a double boiler, place the cream, egg yolk, and honey. Add the flour gradually to prevent lumping. Mix thoroughly. Cook over boiling water, stirring constantly. When the mixture begins to thicken, add the lemon juice and cook 2 to 3 minutes more. Remove from the heat. Serve hot. Excellent on fowl dressing, meats, and Fried Biscuits (see page 29). *Makes 1½ cups.*

VARIATIONS: For *Molasses Gravy*, substitute molasses for honey and add 1 extra tablespoon molasses.

For *Maple Syrup Gravy*, substitute maple syrup for honey and add 1 tablespoon maple syrup.

HUCKLEBERRY JAM GRAVY

*T*his was a favorite of Grandpa Ned's. He loved it especially with corn bread dressing and turkey or hen, but also enjoyed it with biscuits and with cornpone. Said it made him "jolly."

FIREPLACE RECIPE:

Take a jar of huckleberry jam, put with it a little water, a dollop of butter, and a little flour. Cook and stir all together until thick as wanted.

MODERN METHOD:

1   (6-ounce) jar huckleberry
    or blueberry jam (or any tart
    berry jam)

$^1/_2$ cup hot water
1   tablespoon cornstarch
1   tablespoon butter or margarine, melted

In a saucepan, mix the jam and hot water thoroughly. Mix the cornstarch with a little cold water until smooth, and blend into the jam mixture. Place over low heat and cook until juice slightly coats a spoon. Blend in the butter. A tasty addition to most any food. *Makes 1$^1/_2$ cups.*

❧ WHITE GRAVY ❧

*T*his recipe was handed down from generation to generation. It is said that many families in the South dined on
biscuits and White Gravy seven nights a week after the Civil War
ended and their Confederate money became worthless.

FIREPLACE RECIPE:

Put a little flour in pan with meat grease, add milk in amount gravy wanted, cook
till thick as wanted, add salt and pepper.

MODERN METHOD:

4	tablespoons bacon drippings or butter	$^1/_4$	teaspoon salt
4	tablespoons flour	$^1/_4$	teaspoon black pepper
2	cups milk		

In a heavy iron frying pan, heat the bacon drippings or butter over low heat and blend in
the flour. Add the milk gradually, stirring until smooth after each addition. Cook over low
heat until as thick as desired, stirring constantly. Add the salt and pepper. Serve piping hot.
Good over ordinary biscuits. *Makes 2 cups.*

THE COMPLEXION

Bathing it in water in which orange skins have been boiled will
give a fresh appearance.

—From *The Housekeeper Cook Book* (1894)

❧ NASTURTIUM GRAVY ❧

*G*randma had a knack for making new dishes from everyday ingredients. This was her favorite gravy to accom-
pany lowly peas or beans, as well as Sunday chicken or fish.

FIREPLACE RECIPE:

Mix butter and flour, amount needed for a bowl of gravy, and cook in spider pan
over very low coals until the color of light mahogany and no more. Put in a pint of
meat stock with a little vinegar, cook and stir all until smooth. To this put a handful
of nasturtium leaves, a bit of onion grated or chopped, a dash of salt, a pinch of pepper, a spoon of honey, and simmer till of a good color and taste.

MODERN METHOD:

4	tablespoons butter or margarine	2	tablespoons chopped onion
4	tablespoons flour	1	tablespoon honey
$\frac{1}{4}$	cup cider vinegar	$\frac{1}{8}$	teaspoon pepper
$1\frac{3}{4}$	cup meat stock or low-sodium		Salt
	canned beef broth		
$\frac{1}{2}$	cup nasturtium leaves,		
	finely chopped and packed		

In a saucepan or frying pan, melt the butter, add the flour, and cook the roux over very low
heat until light brown. Mix the vinegar with the meat stock, and gradually blend the stock
into the roux, stirring constantly to prevent lumping. Add the nasturtium leaves, onion,
honey, and pepper. Add the salt to taste. Simmer until the gravy reaches the desired consistency. Strain if desired. Best on fowl or fish. Good on vegetables, especially peas and beans.
Makes about 2 cups.

CARROT GRAVY

*G*randma said carrots were supposed to add brightness to your eyes and sweetness to your smile as you grow old. But she contended when you get old, you're just like you always were, only more so.

FIREPLACE RECIPE:

Melt a little butter in a pan and add 2 or 3 carrots finely grated. Put in a little flour and a few sprigs of chopped parsley and some beef stock. Simmer till carrots are tender, mash or run through sieve. Use hot.

MODERN METHOD:

2   tablespoons butter or margarine
1/2   cup finely grated fresh carrots
1   tablespoon flour

1   cup beef stock
1   tablespoon finely chopped parsley (optional)

In a saucepan over low heat, melt the butter. Add the carrots. Blend in the flour with the beef stock, and add the chopped parsley if using. Cook over low heat until the carrots are very tender. If the liquid has cooked down, add a little more beef stock. The gravy should be thin. Run the mixture through a sieve and reheat to serve hot. Gives a new taste to peas, beans, and meats. *Makes about 1 cup.*

⊱ SAWMILL GRAVY ⊰

*G*randpa put together a "crystal radio kit" he ordered from the government. With the wire wrapped around the oatmeal box and everything connected as instructed, he heard a voice from thirty miles out into the world. To celebrate, Grandma treated him to one of his favorite suppers—plain boiled rice covered with plenty of Sawmill Gravy, chicken-fried fatback, and, of course, a plate of fat steaming biscuits with fresh-churned butter.

FIREPLACE RECIPE:

Slice salt meat or smokehouse bacon, lay in spider pan over medium hot coals, and fry. Take up meat and cool drippings. Put to this a little cornmeal and put back on coals of low heat and stir mightily until brown. A tad of vinegar may be liked. Pour in some milk, stirring quick till it thickens, more milk to make thinner if wanted. After sprinkling with pepper, take to table hot. Good over rice, biscuits, or potatoes.

MODERN METHOD:

2 tablespoons bacon drippings	$^1/_8$ teaspoon pepper
4 tablespoons cornmeal	Salt
2 cups milk	$^1/_2$ to $^3/_4$ teaspoon vinegar (optional)

Place a saucepan with the bacon drippings on medium heat. Add the cornmeal and stir until golden brown. Blend in the milk, stirring constantly until it thickens to prevent lumping. Add additional milk to thin if desired. Add the pepper. Taste for seasoning. Drippings usually make it plenty salty. Add your favorite vinegar if desired. Good served over hot biscuits, rice, mashed potatoes, or meats. *Makes about 2 cups.*

❧ SAGE GRAVY ❧

Fido and Rover sniffed this gravy and crawled back under the house. Grandpa wouldn't even taste it, saying, "If it's not good enough for the dogs, it's not good enough for me." Everyone else loved it, of course.

FIREPLACE RECIPE:

Melt a little butter in a pan. Chop fine a handful of green sage leaves and a small onion and add. Mix in a little vinegar. Beat smooth some thickening flour with as much meat broth as gravy needed and simmer till all is tender. Salt and pepper it.

MODERN METHOD:

2	tablespoons butter or margarine	1	tablespoon flour
$1/3$	cup green sage leaves	$1\frac{1}{2}$	cups meat broth
$1/3$	cup grated onion	1	teaspoon salt
2	teaspoons vinegar	$1/2$	teaspoon black pepper

In a stew pan over low heat, melt the butter. Add the sage leaves, onion, and vinegar. Mix the flour with the meat broth and add it to the stew pan. Add the salt and pepper. Simmer until all is tender. Serve as is or strain. Serve hot. *Makes 1³/4 cups.*

GARGLE FOR A SORE THROAT

Take a large handful of red sage (not the common garden sage), boil it in one quart of the best white-wine vinegar, to a near pint, then sweeten it well with honey. You may, if you please, add two small wine-glasses of port wine.

—From *Mackenzie's Five Thousand Receipts* (1852)

GINGERSNAP GRAVY

*A*unt Hattie always had a few gingersnaps left in the cookie jar. When she cooked roast beef, she got them out and made this gravy, saying it made the beef fit for a king.

FIREPLACE RECIPE:

Take a spider pan with a little butter and cook tender a handful of very fine-cut onion over slow fire. Remove. Let wait. Put to butter left in pan a dash of flour and stir till tan. Mix a pint of meat stock with some sharp vinegar and a spoon of honey. Put same of flour and keep the stir.

Now to it put the onions and a handful of gingersnaps, crushed to a crumble. Mix smooth, cook a little longer and it is ready. A few spoons of muscadine wine may be added. Take to the table hot. Best on beef.

MODERN METHOD:

$1/2$ cup finely diced onions

2 tablespoons butter or margarine

1 tablespoon flour

$1/4$ cup cider vinegar

1 cup meat stock or canned beef broth or hot water

$1/2$ cup brown sugar, packed, or 2 tablespoons honey

2 teaspoons lemon juice

6 large (4-inch) gingersnaps, crushed

$1/4$ cup red wine (optional, to sharpen flavor)

In a heavy frying pan, sauté the onions in the butter. Remove the onions and drain as dry as possible. Set the onions aside, but leave the butter in the pan.

To the butter, add the flour. Set on low heat and brown very lightly. Cooking too dark distorts the taste.

Mix the vinegar with the meat stock, and add a little at a time to the flour roux while stirring constantly. Cook until smooth. Blend in the sugar, lemon juice, and gingersnap crumbs, and stir to a boil. Lower the heat, add the onions, and simmer till the mixture begins to thicken. Add the wine, if using. Do not make the gravy too thick—the gingersnaps will make the gravy pleasingly lumpy. Pour over meats. Also tasty on leafy vegetables, especially boiled cabbage. *Makes $1^3/4$ cups.*

❦ SAUSAGE GRAVY ❧

*G*reat-Aunt Vada Mae confessed she made a big mistake when she told her grandchildren this gravy was made from ground-up pigtails mixed with his squeal. She never got them to even taste it.

FIREPLACE RECIPE:

Take a double-handful of fresh ground hog sausage, sprinkle heavy with sage, about 2 spoonfuls, to taste, 1/2 spoon salt, half that of ground red pepper, 2 or 3 dashes freshly ground black pepper. Mix all up well together.

Put in spider, mashing to crumbles as it fries to keep out lumps. When done take up and let wait. Do not brown.

Stir in meat grease a little flour, amount for gravy, put on slow coals and stir till flour cooks to a bubble. Take away and pour in milk, about a quart, and stir till smooth, then add sausage to heat through. Serve steaming over split hot biscuits.

MODERN METHOD:

1 pound seasoned pork sausage, hot*	1/4 cup plus 2 teaspoons all-purpose flour
1 1/2 teaspoons sage	4 cups nonfat milk
1/2 teaspoon salt	

Place the sausage in a frying pan over medium-low heat, continually mashing with a fork as it cooks to keep it in crumbles. Do not let it lump. Remove from the pan when done but not brown.

Mix the sage and salt with the flour. Place in the frying pan with all the drippings and cook to a low bubble. Do not brown. Remove from the heat and add the milk, a little at a time, stirring smooth after each addition. Return to low heat and stir until thick as desired; the gravy should be fairly thin. Add the sausage and cook till piping hot. Remove and skim off as much grease as possible, or lay a paper towel lightly atop the gravy to absorb the grease. Trash the towel and serve the gravy over biscuits or toast. *Makes about 4 cups*.

*If you prefer, use regular seasoned sausage, and add red and black pepper as desired.

⤙ COFFEE SAUCE ⤚

*D*uring sweet potato digging time, every household was overstocked with potatoes. Grandma fried them, cooked them with sautéed onions or pecans, made them into pies, and served them various other ways until the family refused them. Then she whetted their appetites by coming up with a dessert of mashed potatoes covered with this sauce.

FIREPLACE RECIPE:

Take a sack with a half of a cup of nicely roasted and finely ground coffee and drop it in the coffee pot with a pint of water. Boil about 10 minutes, take out coffee sack and while hot, put in a raw egg to settle stray grounds. Add a pinch of salt and set aside a few minutes to settle. Remove egg and it is ready. Use part for sauce, balance for drinking.

Make sauce as thus: Take a quarter pint of coffee and mix with half as much sugar, dash in a few grains of salt, a pinch of flour, and mix with 2 eggs beaten to one color. Cook in patty pan over water until thick as wished. Cool. Stir in frothed sweet cream when ready to serve. Pour over creamed sweet potatoes.

MODERN METHOD:

$1/4$ cup plus 1 teaspoon sugar	$1/2$ cup very strong hot coffee
1 teaspoon flour	2 eggs, beaten
(optional, for a thicker sauce)	$3/4$ cup whipped cream
$1/4$ teaspoon salt	

In the top of a double boiler, combine all the sugar, flour (if using), and salt. Stir in the hot coffee until smooth and not grainy. Heat, but not to boiling.

Place the beaten eggs in a saucepan, and pour half the hot liquid by the spoonfuls onto the beaten eggs while stirring constantly. Add the egg mixture back to the liquid in the top of the double boiler and mix well.

Place the top of the double boiler over simmering water, and cook while stirring until the mixture slightly coats the spoon. Remove from the heat. Chill. When ready to serve, fold in the whipped cream. Excellent on mashed sweet potatoes or yams. *Makes about 1 cup.*

BEET SAUCE DRESSING WITH BEETS

*G*randpa loved ruby red color. Grandma usually had either steamed dried beets or fresh beets on the table, sometimes pickled, sometimes pepper-sauced, and sometimes plain boiled. When she covered them with this dressing, she said that as he was leaving the table, he stooped and kissed the back of her neck. Needless to say, she cooked it often.

FIREPLACE RECIPE:

Wash and scrub beets for a pint fine cut, put to saucepan and cover with clear water. Clean and scrape horseradish root and of this grate fine a small handful to which put a little more than equal amount of sugar, and $1/4$ pint good cider vinegar. Put the whole to beets. Tender beets in a slow simmer and remove from fire. Drain liquid for sauce.

Put in skillet over low heat a mix of a little butter, same of flour, salt and pepper, and stir in beet draining of a half-pint. Cook while stirring till slightly thick. Stir in a pinch or two of dry mustard. Pour over beets.

MODERN METHOD:

$1/2$ cup cider vinegar	2 tablespoons flour
$3/4$ cup sugar	$1/2$ teaspoon salt
2 teaspoons pure horseradish	$1/4$ teaspoon black pepper
2 cups beets, washed, scraped (or peeled), and finely chopped	1 cup beet water
2 tablespoons butter	$1/4$ teaspoon dry mustard

In a saucepan, blend the vinegar and sugar; add the horseradish and beets. Barely cover the beets with water, and slow-simmer until the beets are tender. Remove from the heat. Pour off the liquid and save 1 cup for the sauce. Place the beets in a serving dish to keep warm.

In a frying pan, melt the butter and add the flour, salt, and pepper; stir well. Blend in the 1 cup beet water. Stir until smooth. Simmer over very low heat, stirring constantly, until the mixture begins to thicken. Remove from the heat while the mixture is still thin. Add the mustard, mix thoroughly, and pour over the beets. Serve warm with meats or fish. *Makes 6 servings.*

∽ CREAM DRESSING ∽

*W*hile the menfolk were on a daybreak squirrel hunt, Aunt Willie Mae made up biscuits and readied ingredients for Cream Dressing to go over the fried squirrel. When the fellows returned and skinned and dressed the squirrels, all she had to do to prepare breakfast was bake biscuits while the squirrels were frying, then cook the dressing.

FIREPLACE RECIPE:

In patty pan, put together spices, a little of each, mustard, salt and sugar, and a pinch of cayenne, all to taste, and put a spoon or two of flour for thickening. Put in a frothed egg, some milk with cream, in the quantity of dressing wanted. Mix in a little vinegar. Set in Dutch oven with water. Cook over medium coals till thick, stirring, then put in a little melted butter. When done, spoon over squirrel, vegetables, or meats.

MODERN METHOD:

1	tablespoon flour		Few grains of cayenne
2	teaspoons cornstarch	1	egg
1	teaspoon salt	1	cup cream or half-and-half
2	teaspoons sugar	3	tablespoons cider vinegar
1/2	teaspoon dry mustard	2	tablespoons butter or margarine

In the top of a double boiler, sift together the flour, cornstarch, salt, sugar, mustard, and cayenne. In a separate small bowl, beat the egg well and blend in the cream. Add the egg mixture to the flour mixture a little at a time, mixing thoroughly. Cook over simmering water, stirring constantly until the mixture begins to thicken; add the vinegar. Cook to the desired consistency. Remove from the heat. Blend in the butter. Serve hot over vegetables or meat. *Makes 1 1/4 cups.*

VARIATIONS: For different flavors, add 1 tablespoon or more grated onion, grated horseradish, chopped parsley, or grated cheese. Or you can substitute tarragon vinegar for cider vinegar, or use a combination of the two vinegars to taste.

❦ CIDER MINT SAUCE ❧

*W*hile Grandpa was at the creek fishing for catfish, Grandma was usually making the sauce he loved to douse them with at the table. One day he came home swinging a string of eels, and she politely took them outside as if to dress them. Instead, she sent them sailing over the back fence into the woods. Luckily, he also liked the sauce on Corn Fritters (see page 77).

FIREPLACE RECIPE:

Heat in boiler over slow coals a pint of water, a quarter pint of finest sugar, a little thickening, a short pint of apple cider, and a stirring spoon full of cider vinegar. Then put in a little honey and a dash or two of salt and a smidgen of pepper.

Mix all well together and bring to a bubble over fire, then put in a handful of peppermint leaves. Simmer down to half and remove. Strain through wet muslin. Especially good with fish, but adds to lamb or any meat.

MODERN METHOD:

1 cup boiling water
1/2 cup peppermint leaves
    packed, finely chopped*
1/4 cup sugar, or to taste
1 teaspoon honey
2/3 cup apple cider

1 tablespoon cider vinegar
1/2 teaspoon salt
1/8 teaspoon pepper
1 tablespoon flour
1/2 tablespoon cornstarch

In a saucepan, pour the boiling water over the mint leaves. Let stand 1 hour or more, strain, and discard the leaves. To the water, add the sugar, honey, apple cider, vinegar, salt, and pepper. Add slowly to a mix of the flour and cornstarch. Simmer over low heat, stirring constantly, until the liquid is reduced, but do not cook until thick; the mixture should be thin. Remove from the heat. Serve warm. May be made in advance and reheated. Very good when a tart sauce is desired. *Makes about 2 cups.*

*4 drops peppermint oil may be used instead of mint leaves.

⤳ SUGAR VINEGAR ⤳

The general store was miles away from Grandma's and sometimes it was weeks between her visits. Since ingredients for cooking were to a great extent limited to those in the garden and woods, she had to learn to make her own. This is not the first recipe she concocted trying to make this vinegar, but it turned out so good, it was the last. She passed it around to all the relatives.

FIREPLACE RECIPE:

To make a good sugar vinegar, put 1 quart sugar, 7 quarts water, and a good big mother* in a stone jar and set in a warm place till fermentation.

MODERN METHOD:

The same basic recipe is used today.

*Yeast cells that form on the surface of fermenting liquid to start production of vinegar. This sediment was spooned off the top of an older bowl of vinegar.

RECIPE FOR CLEANING DELICATE VALUABLES

Use leavened bread to clean dirt and dust from old book covers without affecting original color or lettering.

Hold a good size piece of bread firmly in hand and rub book covers till bread finely crumbles and is of no further use. Destroy. Thorough cleaning may take several pieces.

With new bread in hand, mash covers tightly together and rub page ends. Cleans staleness from their long existence.

Likewise, clean coats of age from other delicate valuables.

—Handwritten on a lone sheet of paper found in one of Grandma Grace's receipt books. (It may have been written after sliced bread became popular.)

⤳ CELERY VINEGAR ⤳

*T*his is another of Grandma's concoctions that caught on with the family.

FIREPLACE RECIPE:

Wrap handful of celery seed in stout muslin or double thinner cloth and pound into mortar. Boil a hefty pint of best vinegar, cool, and pour over mortar. After a fortnight, strain and bottle.

MODERN METHOD:

1   tablespoon plus 1 teaspoon celery seed*
1   cup vinegar

Place the celery seed in a thick cloth. Beat until as powdery as possible and empty into a jar. Boil the vinegar and when cool, pour over the powdered seeds. Cover. Let sit 2 weeks before using. Spoon over table-ready beef or pork. Also a good dressing for green salads. *Makes about 1 cup.*

*If stronger taste is desired, add additional seeds.

SASSAFRAS

We are informed that in many parts of America, where sassafras trees not only grow in great numbers in the woods, but are planted along the fences of inclosures. It is not unusual to make bed-posts of the wood for the purpose of expelling bugs. Its powerful scent drives away these disagreeable insects; and some persons put chips of sassafras in their wardrobes and chests, to prevent the attack of moths.

—From *Useful Knowledge* by Reverend William Bingley (1818)

∾ NUTMEG SPREADING SAUCE ∾

*A*nnie Belle was a teacher in the school in Grandma's area. She loved literature and told of many romantic legends from centuries back that involved nutmeg. One custom she followed was to carry a nutmeg ball in a lace handkerchief for good luck in marriage. Later she said it worked like a charm, concocted this recipe, and passed it around.

FIREPLACE RECIPE:

To make a good sauce for any kind of pudding or pie, take 4 big spoonfuls of fresh-churned butter and put with it some sugar, 6 big spoons, and half of a grated nutmeg. Bring to one quick boil and take from fire. Nice served on puddings and cakes at any temperature.

MODERN METHOD:

$1/2$ cup butter or margarine
$1/2$ plus $1/2$ cup confectioners' sugar
1   plus 1 tablespoons water
$1/4$ teaspoon ground nutmeg plus $1/4$ teaspoon for topping

Beat the butter in a bowl until creamy. Add $1/2$ cup sugar and 1 tablespoon water. Beat well and add the remaining $1/2$ cup sugar and the remaining 1 tablespoon water. Beat until smooth. When light and fluffy, add $1/4$ teaspoon nutmeg or to taste. Heat to the boiling point. At the first bubble, quickly remove from the heat. Spread as a topping over pudding, cakes, or tea cakes. Lightly sprinkle the top with the remaining $1/4$ teaspoon nutmeg. *Makes $1/2$ cup.*

∽ WATERMELON SYRUP ∽

A big "to do" was held at the church every Fourth of July. Among the games were sack races, greased pig races, and horseshoe pitching, but the main event was a watermelon-eating contest. That red juice dripping from the kids' elbows inspired Grandma to concoct this goody to pour over her Bread Pudding (see page 176).

FIREPLACE RECIPE:

Run heart watermelon through sieve for one gallon pulp and juice, and simmer this down over slow coals to one quart. Skim as necessary. Add 2 or 3 big spoons of sugar and cook juice down till tasty as suits. Especially good on bread pudding or flapjacks.

MODERN METHOD:

2 quarts seeded, ripe, watermelon pulp, puréed
$^1/_4$ cup sugar, or to taste

Scrape enough red watermelon meat to make 2 quarts of pulp and juice after pressing it through a coarse strainer. Over simmering heat, cook about an hour, add the sugar, and mix well. Slow-simmer until the mixture is slightly thickened. Taste for desired sweetness. Adjust by adding sugar or a little water. Takes 3 or 4 hours cooking time. Good as a topping for Bread Pudding (see page 176) or as a substitute for maple syrup on Flapjacks (see page 40). *Makes 4 to 5 cups.*

HONEY WATER FOR THE HAIR

Take of honey, 4 lbs. very dry sand, 2 lbs. Mix and put into a vessel that will hold five times as much; distil with a gentle heat a yellowish acid water: this acid greatly encourages the growth of hair.

—From *Mackenzie's Five Thousand Receipts* (1852)

❧ FRIED SYRUP ❧

*I*t was good manners for anyone visiting near mealtime to stay to dine. When the veterinarian came to attend Grandpa's sick horse, Grandma prepared her famous quick meal of Fried Syrup and Flapjacks (see page 40), along with fried ham accompanied by plenty of strong coffee.

FIREPLACE RECIPE:

Lay a few good size cured, hickory-smoked ham slices in the spider and fry over medium hot coals till both sides are very brown. Take up and pour in a quarter pint or so of hot water, scrape all ham leavings from sides and bottom, and give it a boil. Gradually stir in sugarcane molasses as liked, and mix the whole well together. Let come to a full bubble and remove from heat. When cool, pour over flapjacks or golden hot biscuits. Serve with the ham.

MODERN METHOD:

1   (1-inch) center-slice smoked ham, about 1$^1/_2$ pounds, trimmed
1   tablespoon butter or margarine
$^1/_2$ cup hot water
$^3/_4$ cup sugarcane molasses or other pure molasses

Cut the ham into four pieces. Place in a heavy skillet containing the butter and fry until done and well browned on both sides. Do not burn. Remove from the skillet and keep warm.

Scrape all the ham particles from the sides and bottom of the skillet, add the water, and bring to a boil, stirring constantly. Gradually mix in the molasses and stir until well blended. Bring to a boil again and immediately remove from heat. Cool before serving. Good over Flapjacks (see page 40), waffles, or hot biscuits. Serve with the ham. *Makes about 1$^1/_4$ cups.*

TO DESTROY CRICKETS

Put Scotch snuff upon the holes where they come out.

—From *Mackenzie's Five Thousand Receipts* (1852)

❧ SAUSAGE SYRUP ❧

*T*he day Grandma got electricity in her house and could pull a chain and beat the rooster to daylight, she celebrated with a breakfast of Flapjacks (see page 40) and Sausage Syrup.

FIREPLACE RECIPE:

In spider pan, low-fry every drop of grease out of a pint of sausage meat to which there leaves a brown crust. Keep grainy. Do not let chunk. Drain good and put to it a short pint of fresh-made sugarcane molasses and serve warm over hot flapjacks.

MODERN METHOD:

1   pound seasoned pork sausage
1/4   cup hot water

1 1/2 cups sugarcane molasses or maple syrup

Fry the sausage in a pan over low heat, stirring and mashing constantly, so that no lumps will form; the sausage should be grainy. Drain off the fat often, so a little of the sausage will have a brown crust. When done, place the sausage on a paper towel to drain away as much grease as possible.

Discard the grease left in the frying pan, being careful to save all the meat particles. Pour the hot water into the pan, cover, place over low heat, and bring to a simmer to soften the browned particles. Scrape the sides of the pan to get all particles. Simmer until smooth and then add the molasses. Blend in the sausage and bring to a boil. Remove from the heat immediately. Serve in a deep bowl with a dipping spoon, because the syrup is thin and the sausage will sink to the bottom. Serve on Flapjacks or Bread Pudding (see pages 40 and 176), on biscuits, or as desired. *Makes about 2 1/2 cups.*

NOTE: The sausage may be fried in marble-size or pea-size balls, but it takes longer to prepare the balls and to fry them.

MOLASSES "PRESERVES"

*D*uring a visit to old Dr. Smithers, the area physician, Grandma was advised, among other things, that molasses was a good cure for "what ails you." He gave her this recipe and told her to use it at least once a week. From then on, the whole family looked forward to breakfast with Molasses "Preserves."

FIREPLACE RECIPE:

To a pint of molasses, put juice of a lemon and a few gratings of nutmeg in stew pot on trivet over hot coals for a quick boil. Have 4 eggs beaten to one color and pour all at once into boiling molasses, stirring as poured. Remove from fire quickly and take to table with a plate of hot biscuits and a round of fresh-churned butter.

MODERN METHOD:

2 cups sugarcane molasses	$^1/_2$ teaspoon nutmeg, if desired	
3 tablespoons lemon juice	4 eggs, thoroughly beaten	

Simmer the molasses about 10 minutes. Add the lemon juice and nutmeg and bring to a rolling boil. Pour the eggs all at once into the boiling molasses, stirring briskly to separate the eggs into small pieces. Immediately remove from the heat. Serve when cool, but not cold, with hot, generously buttered biscuits or over fresh, crisp toast. *Makes 4 servings.*

FIRE KINDLERS

To make very nice fire kindlers, take rosin, any quantity, melt it, putting in for each pound being used, from 2 to 3 oz. of tallow, and when all is hot, stir in pure saw-dust to make very thick; and, while yet hot, spread it out about 1 inch thick, upon boards which have fine saw-dust sprinkled upon them, to prevent it from sticking.

—From *Dr. Chase's Recipes* (1867)

Jams, Jellies, and Preserves

∽ CARROT JAM ∽

*G*randma loved the yellow smell of carrots. Taking the time to make Carrot Jam was one way she got rid of her "all-overs," a bad feeling that didn't hurt in any particular place—it was just there.

FIREPLACE RECIPE:

In sufficient pot, chip fine or run through coarse chopper carrots peeled of about a quart or more, and to this put a red apple or two cored and peeled and chopped rather coarse. Water cover. Then put in a big handful of raisins run through the chopper, and two lemons peeled and sliced thin as possible but with no pith. Simmer all to tender carrots a little. Put with this about a pint good sugar, a half-pint good fresh clover honey, and a few gratings of nutmeg. Slow boil over medium heat until a little liquid in the spoon falls back into pot in one drop as with jelly. But not too long, otherwise it will not fix. Seal in small jars.

MODERN METHOD:

5	cups peeled and cubed (1-inch) carrots	3/4 cup raisins
2	small lemons, peeled and thinly sliced	1/4 teaspoon nutmeg
1	cup peeled, cored, and coarsely chopped cooking apples (2 medium)	2 cups sugar
		1 cup honey

Place the carrots, lemons, apples, raisins, and nutmeg in a saucepan. Barely cover with water. Cover and slow-boil about 20 to 25 minutes until the carrots are tender. Set aside until cool. Then add the sugar and honey and mix well. Simmer uncovered on medium heat about 30 minutes, stirring often until the liquid is at jelly stage; a few drops on a plate should stay in place.

Remove from the heat and mash the carrots with a fork, or place in a blender on low speed for a short time. Leave tiny chunks. The mixture will thicken when cool. Place in sterile canning jars and seal. *Makes about 2 1/2 pints.*

WATERMELON JAM

*A*t the end of watermelon season, everyone had forgotten the excitement of the first ripe watermelon in early June and was tired of the sweet, juicy, red meat. Ripe melons lay in the field sunburning and drying up. Grandma never liked seeing food go to waste, so she canned as many melons as she could in a variety of ways, this jam being one of her favorites.

FIREPLACE RECIPE:

Take red meat of duly ripe watermelon with a little white rind, cut in thumb-size pieces, and thinly slice a lemon or two over this. Mix and put in tighten jar which place in water bucket and lower into well to stay cool.

Next morning place melon in kettle, hang over edge of slow coals with a smidgen less than half as much sugar as watermelon, and cook several hours until it thickens. Pull forward occasionally to stir. When done, add a little spirits to taste and cook a little longer. Seal hot in jars.

MODERN METHOD:

8   cups prepared watermelon (see directions below), about half an average-size melon
2   small lemons, thinly sliced
3$\frac{1}{2}$ cups sugar
$\frac{1}{4}$ to $\frac{1}{2}$ cup rum, brandy, or spirits as desired

Cut the red meat of the watermelon and a cup of the white rind into thumb-size pieces, and place into a noncorrosive bowl. Add the lemons, mix, cover, and set in a cool place until the next day. Stir lightly a time or two to turn over the ingredients.

Place the melon in an open saucepan, add the sugar, and cook very slowly several hours until it thickens to suit, stirring lightly. White rind makes small lumps, as in other types of jam. They will be transparent and may be mashed smaller.

Just before taking the jam out of the saucepan, add the spirits and simmer about 5 minutes more. While hot, place in sterile canning jars and seal. *Makes 2 to 3 cups.*

☙ SCUPPERNONG HULL JAM ❧

*T*he donkey Cousin Ellie ordered from Sears Roebuck came by train and was delivered by the depot agent. A few days after its arrival, Ellie gave a big party to celebrate her son's return from the war. The kids were promised a donkey ride, but didn't get it because the donkey (named Whoa) balked. Ellie eased their disappointment with her jam-filled biscuits.

FIREPLACE RECIPE:

Take 1 quart scuppernongs, squeeze out pulp, discard seeds, and set pulp aside with juice. Put hulls in water in large stew pot and boil on medium coals until tender. Drain and compress. Add pulp and juice, several slices of lemon, and a little water. Boil together a pint and a little more of sugar till juice thickens. It is done.

MODERN METHOD:

4 cups raw scuppernongs or tough-skinned grapes	3 cups sugar
	$1/4$ lemon, thinly sliced

Mash the pulp from the grapes, and remove the seeds by rubbing the pulp through a sieve. Discard the seeds. Set aside the pulp and juice.

In a heavy saucepan, cover the grape hulls with water, boil until tender, drain well, and mash to pieces with a fork or potato masher. Some hulls will not be very tender and will be left whole or in halves, making the jam pleasantly chewy.

To the hulls, add the pulp, juice, sugar, lemon slices, and a little water if necessary to make about 3 cups. Boil the mixture over medium heat, stirring frequently until the juice thickens, usually 15 to 25 minutes. Remove from the heat when the juice forms a soft ball in cold water. Can in sterile jars, while hot. This is an excellent sandwich filling. *Makes $1\frac{1}{2}$ to 2 pints.*

VARIATIONS: For different sandwich fillings, mix Scuppernong Hull Jam with peanut butter to form a lumpy paste, or sprinkle the jam with roasted peanuts chopped to bits.

❧ BEET PRESERVES ❧

*U*ncle J.D. loved Grandma's preserved beets, especially with chicken and dressing. Juice ran around the edge of his plate for a fine, colorful garnish.

FIREPLACE RECIPE:

Take beets to make a pint and wash thoroughly. Cut into finger size sticks and boil in water in stew pan a few minutes. Pour away all water except as covers beets. Add as much sugar as beets and a half tea-cup of good cane molasses. To this put lemons with juice and rind to taste. Cook over slow fire about one hour or until juice is thick as wanted, stirring often but not so swift as to mangle beets. Throw in a handful of pecan meats and cook a little more. Serve with meat or chicken dressing or other.

MODERN METHOD:

2	cups beets, cut into thin strips, about 1 pound raw	2	medium lemons, thinly sliced
2	cups sugar	1	teaspoon grated lemon rind
1/4	cup sugarcane molasses	1	cup pecans, coarsely chopped (walnuts may be used)

Wash the beets thoroughly and slice them, unpeeled, into thin strips as for shoestring french fries. Cover with water and boil 15 minutes. Drain. Pour back enough water to cover the beets, and save the excess in another container.

To the beets and water, add the sugar, molasses, lemons, and lemon rind. Mix thoroughly. Bring to a boil, and then simmer the mix about an hour until the beets are tender and the juice is properly thickened. Stir often. Some strips will be broken, but do not mush. Add the nuts and cook 5 minutes or more. Seal in small or ½-pint sterile jars. Good on biscuits or as a substitute for cranberry jelly with fowl dressing. *Makes about 6 pints.*

NOTE: The saved beet water is nutritious and may be diluted and served as pink iced tea.

⊂⊃ WATERMELON RIND ⊂⊃ PRESERVES

*G*randma had no qualms about learning new recipes by listening to conversations on her eight-party telephone line. On this recipe she wrote, "From the grapevine."

FIREPLACE RECIPE:

Slice thin or cut in small squares a quart of watermelon rind from which green hull and pink have been removed, and sink in a crock with salted water and let rest overnight.

Come morning, drain off brine and place in stew pan with new water; add a pinch of alum and set it over a quick fire and boil a few minutes, 15 will do it, then drain and rinse.

Put together a scant pint of new water with a pint of sugar and a little lemon as suits in kettle and boil to thin syrup, and to this put the rind. Give all a long simmer over slow fire till rind is glass clear and can be pierced with a straw. Pack in Mason jars with syrup.

MODERN METHOD:

4 cups white part of watermelon rind, cubed, about one-quarter of a large melon

$^1/_4$ cup salt in 1 quart water for soaking brine

$^1/_8$ teaspoon alum

2 cups sugar

$1^3/_4$ cups water

$^1/_2$ lemon, thinly sliced, or more to taste

From the watermelon rind, cut away all the green and pink and discard. Dice the white rind into 1-inch cubes, and place in the salt solution in a noncorrosive pan to stand overnight. Next morning, drain and rinse thoroughly with cold water. Cover the rind with fresh water, add the alum, and boil 15 minutes. Drain and rinse well.

In a heavy pot, combine the sugar, $1^3/_4$ cups water, and lemon slices, and boil to a thin syrup, about 5 minutes. Skim, if necessary. Add the rind, bring to a boil, and simmer about 45 minutes, or until the rind is tender and translucent. Remove from the heat, and place in sterile jars with the juice to within 1 inch of the top, or let sit in the juice about 3 days before using. *Makes 2 pints.*

VARIATION: For a tasty and colorful holiday garnish for fowl dressing or other dressings, divide the rinds into batches according to the number of colors desired. Place each batch in a separate sterile jar and add red, green, or other food coloring to the juice.

GARLIC, TO GLUE BROKEN GLASS

It has a very acrid taste, and a highly offensive smell, which pervade the whole plant. When bruised and applied to the skin, it causes inflamation, and raises blisters.

The medical properties of garlic are various. In dropsical complaints, asthmas, and agues, it is said to have been successfully used. Some instances have occurred, in deafness, of the beneficial effects of wrapping a clove of garlic in muslin and putting it into the ear.

An oil is sometimes prepared from garlic which is so heavy as to sink in water; but the virtues of this pungent vegetable are more perfectly and more readily extracted by spirit of wine than any other way. A syrup is also made from it.

The juice of garlic is said to be the best and strongest cement that can be adopted for broken glass and china, leaving little or no mark, if used with care.

—From *Useful Knowledge* by Reverend William Bingley (1818)

❧ TUESDAY'S LEMON JELLY ❧

*W*hen Grandma was young, she wanted to become a nurse, but in her day families did not believe in educating girls because their place was in the home being a mother. With plenty of time on her hands, she spent much of it experimenting with food, such as this jelly. After many tries, she finally made it to suit her taste on a Tuesday—hence the name "Tuesday's Lemon Jelly."

FIREPLACE RECIPE:

To the juice of 4 or so lemons and a little grated rind, add sugar, about a hefty cup. Boil it pretty quick over a clear fire till it jellies, which is known by dipping a spoon into the liquid and holding it in the air; when it hangs to the spoon in a drop, it is done.

The last 2 or 3 minutes, add several lemon verbena leaves and remove when done. If the jelly is boiled too long, it will lose its flavor and shrink very much.

MODERN METHOD:

$2/3$ cup lemon juice

1 tablespoon grated rind

1 cup sugar

3 medium lemon verbena leaves

In a noncorrosive pan, mix the lemon juice and grated rind. Cook uncovered about 3 minutes and add the sugar. Simmer over low heat, stirring constantly, about 5 minutes. Then begin testing for the jelly stage, which is reached when 2 large drops falling from the side of the spoon merge into 1 drop, or when the mixture forms a soft ball in cold water. During the last few minutes of cooking, add the verbena leaves. Remove from the heat at the jelly stage, and discard the verbena leaves. Can in a sterile jar. Small batches do best. Good served with chicken or turkey dressing, baked ham, or most any meat. *Makes about ½ pint.*

☙ SAIDIE'S MARIGOLD JELLY ☙

*C*ousin Saidie had some petals left over after making a marigold pack for Uncle Fred's "shingle-itch" around his waist, which forced him to wear her tent dresses. She threw the leftover petals into her jelly and swore they made it taste better than ever.

FIREPLACE RECIPE:

Take equal amounts of pure pulp from oranges and lemons and put to this two times that amount of water and let stand.

Next day put to saucepan on trivet over fast coals and roll a boil a few minutes, then let stand till the following day. Add equal amount of the best white sugar, then a few marigold petals and cook to jelly. Take out petals and jar.

MODERN METHOD:

3   oranges

3   lemons

2   cups sugar (depending on amount of fruit)

8   marigold petals from outside of flower (these are strongest)

Prepare the fruit using only the segments clear of fiber. Chop finely. Add twice the amount of water as fruit, and set this aside for 18 to 24 hours. Place on high heat, boil hard for 1 or 2 minutes, and set aside for another 18 to 24 hours.

Add an amount of sugar equal to the amount of fruit mix, along with the marigold petals, and boil briskly until the jelly stage is reached, that is, until 2 large drops on the edge of a spoon form 1 drop that hesitates to fall. Take care not to let the mix scorch. Remove from the heat and discard the petals. Pour into sterile jelly glasses and seal. The jelly will not be clear. Best eaten when cold, this jelly has an unusual flavor, unlike any other. Excellent with Fried Biscuits (see page 29). *Makes 1 scant cup.*

☙ PUMPKIN GUMBO ❧

*A*unt Dulcie insisted that Grandma try making a batch of this preserve-like gumbo. She did and liked it, so she put the recipe in her collection for the whole family to enjoy. Grandma said this gumbo was "good, and good for you."

FIREPLACE RECIPE:

Take a small pumpkin, peel and cut up. Mix in some raw apple and as much sugar as pumpkin. Add some thinly sliced lemon and a few raisins. Let set a day and cook till tender. Mash. Best when eaten cold.

MODERN METHOD:

6   cups (1-inch cubes) pumpkin meat
1   cup (1-inch cubes) cooking apple
6   cups sugar
2   lemons, thinly sliced
$1/2$ cup chopped raisins

Place the pumpkin cubes, apple cubes, sugar, lemon slices, and raisins in a saucepan and mix well. Let sit 18 to 24 hours at room temperature. Next day, simmer over low heat until the pumpkin is tender, but not mushy. Remove from the heat. Mash half the pumpkin with a fork until lumpy and return to the heat. Simmer 1 minute more. Best when eaten cold. *Makes about 4 cups.*

SELF-HOLDER FOR A SPOON

In dropping medicine into a spoon, place the handle between leaves of a closed book lying on the table, and then both hands may be used in dropping the mixture.

—From *The Housekeeper Cook Book* (1894)

Relishes and Pickles

⊱ GRAPE CATSUP ⊰

*H*ousewives began making grape (muscadine) catsup to spice up bland dishes after the War Between the States, when gardens had to be re-grown after destruction by Yankee soldiers. Since grapes grew wild, sometimes covering trees, Grandma explained that she would carry a fishing pole to knock the grapes to the ground, where they could be picked up in buckets. After a giggle, she added that Maylee down the road had a healthy, producing internal grape vine. She grew sour grapes.

FIREPLACE RECIPE:

Boil 2 or 3 teacups of grapes till tender. Run through sieve. To the mushy juice, add sugar, vinegar, and spices to taste.

MODERN METHOD:

2	pounds Concord grapes	$^1/_4$	teaspoon salt
2	cups sugar	1	cup vinegar
1	teaspoon each allspice and cloves		Other spices if desired

Boil the grapes 10 to 15 minutes or until tender. Drain. Crush them in a saucepan, and run through a sieve to remove the hulls and seeds. Add the sugar, allspice, cloves, salt, vinegar, and other spices, if using, to the juice. Bring the mixture to a boil, and simmer about 20 minutes or to the desired thickness. Strain and bottle in sterile jars. *Makes 1¾ cups if fairly thick.*

BRUISES

Apply coarse, wet brown paper. It will reduce swelling, and prevent great discolorations.

—From *The Housekeeper Cook Book* (1894)

PEPPER CATSUP

Although years had gone by after the War Between the States, it was hard for southerners to replace vegetable gardens that Yankees had destroyed. This was a recipe that made their dry beans more palatable.

FIREPLACE RECIPE:

Chop a handful of red hot peppers, onion or two, horseradish scrapings, and spice. Boil. Thicken with flour.

MODERN METHOD:

6 large hot red peppers
3 cups vinegar
$1^1/_2$ teaspoons salt
$1^1/_4$ teaspoons grated horseradish

$1^1/_4$ cups chopped onion
$^1/_2$ teaspoon each black pepper and allspice
1 tablespoon flour

Chop the peppers and boil with the vinegar, salt, horseradish, onion, black pepper, and allspice until all the ingredients are soft. Strain and run through a sieve. Add the flour. Boil on low for 5 minutes, stirring constantly. Pour the catsup into sterile jars and seal. *Makes about 3 cups*.

GARDEN CARROT FOR ULCERS

The various uses of the carrot in cooking are well known. But although it contains much nutriment, it is difficult of digestion; particularly if eaten raw, or imperfectly boiled. Carrots are an excellent fodder for cattle and horses, either alone or mixed with hay.

Carrots contain a large portion of saccharine matter, and various but unsuccessful experiments have been made to extract sugar from them.

A marmalade of carrots has been used with success in sea-scurvy, and a poultice prepared from them is sometimes employed in cancerous ulcers.

—From *Useful Knowledge* by Reverend William Bingley (1818)

129

↭ BEER CATSUP ↭

*W*hile Grandma's neighbor was rebuilding his still after Federal Revenuers axed it, he turned to beer concoctions, such as this catsup. He needed to liven up his daily peas and beans. When "white lightning" flowed again, so did the variety of fine food on the dinner table.

FIREPLACE RECIPE:

Take a goodly amount of stale beer, some anchovies and shallots, several handfuls large mushroom flaps chopped, and desired spices. Simmer to half.

MODERN METHOD:

1	quart stale beer	$1/8$	teaspoon cloves
1	cup anchovies	$1/8$	teaspoon red pepper
1	cup shallots	1	tablespoon powdered ginger
$1/8$	teaspoon mace		

Place the beer, anchovies, shallots, mace, cloves, red pepper, and ginger in a saucepan over medium heat. Cover and simmer until reduced by half. Strain through a thick cloth, and bottle in sterile jars when cold. *Makes 3 cups.*

TO PREVENT THE CREAKING OF A DOOR

Rub a bit of soap on the hinges.

—From *Mackenzie's Five Thousand Receipts* (1852)

⮂ GEORGIA CHOWCHOW ⮀

*G*randma said that plain beans or peas on your plate needed a little kick to bring out their flavor, and chowchow was just the ticket.

FIREPLACE RECIPE:

Chop cabbages into very small pieces till a quart. Chop up a few green tomatoes, 2 or 3 healthy green peppers, same of sweet reds, a few onions, and the mix is right. Sprinkle over this ¼ pint of salt in layers, put in sun, a day is a good time, then squeeze in muslin cloth. Put in a boiling kettle a quart of good vinegar with 1½ pints of mixed white and brown sugar. Put vegetables, pinch of mustard seed, and celery seed.

Boil until vegetables are tender but no more. It is finished.

MODERN METHOD:

4	cups shredded head cabbage		Cloth for straining
4	cups chopped sweet onions	1	quart cider vinegar
3	cups chopped green bell peppers	1½	cups granulated sugar
1	cup chopped red bell peppers	1½	cups brown sugar
3	cups chopped green tomatoes	3	tablespoons mustard seed
½	cup salt	2	tablespoons celery seed

In a large bowl, mix the cabbage, onions, green and red peppers, and tomatoes. Divide into three portions. Divide the salt into three portions. Place one portion of the vegetable mixture in a noncorrosive pan and top with one portion of the salt. Repeat these layers using the second and third portions of vegetables and salt (there should be three layers of each, with the salt on top). Allow to remain for 6 to 8 hours or overnight. Drain. Place the vegetables in a cloth, and squeeze to remove all possible juice; discard the juice.

Mix the vinegar and sugars in a saucepan, place over low heat, and bring to a boil Add the vegetables from the cloth along with the mustard seed and celery seed, and cook until all is tender, 10 to 20 minutes. Pour into sterile jars and seal. Let mellow a week before using. *Makes about 2 quarts.*

❦ CORN RELISH ❧

A visitor seldom left Grandma's without a jar of some goody from her wealthy cellar. Aunt Lizzie never stopped praising this relish until the day she went to her reward.

FIREPLACE RECIPE:

Cut the whole grains of corn from roasting ears to make a quart. Do not scrape cob. Put in a kettle and mix in a short pint of unrefined sugar or the same of molasses plus a spoon or two. Chop up two big onions, peppers, a green and a red bell, more if small, a few green tomatoes, and mix in proper salt. Put to this a little celery seed and dry mustard.

Pour over this a quart of good cider vinegar and simmer all in open kettle. Put up in jars.

MODERN METHOD:

2 cups fresh whole-kernel corn*	3/4 cup medium-finely chopped green tomatoes
3/4 cup packed brown sugar	1 teaspoon salt
3/4 cup chopped onion	1 tablespoon celery seed
1 medium green bell pepper, finely chopped	1 teaspoon dry mustard
1 medium red bell pepper, medium-finely chopped	1 quart cider vinegar

Mix the corn, sugar, onion, peppers, tomatoes, salt, celery seed, dry mustard, and vinegar, and bring to a boil. Simmer uncovered 35 to 40 minutes or until the vegetables are tender. Relish should not be very juicy. Eat fresh or can while hot in sterile jars. Serve with meats or vegetables. *Makes 3 to 4 cups.*

*When fresh corn is out of season, substitute a 1-pound package of frozen whole kernel corn.

⤽ GREEN TOMATO RELISH ⤼

*C*utworms got into the stalks of Grandma's tomato plants and left them drooping with green tomatoes. There were so many, she fried a few for dinner and used the balance in this relish.

FIREPLACE RECIPE:

Take a peck of small green tomatoes, stem, wash, and chop same. To this mix 2 quarts onions, peeled and chopped. Sprinkle with salt and let stand overnight. Drain and rinse in new water. In a kettle, pour 2 quarts vinegar. Same of unrefined sugar, a little flour, mustard and celery seed, cloves, allspice, and red pepper powder. Simmer over low fire till all is tender and liquid almost gone. Let set before using.

MODERN METHOD:

4 cups green tomatoes, thinly sliced	2 teaspoons prepared mustard
1 cup chopped onion	2 teaspoons celery seed
$1/3$ cup salt for sprinkling	$1/4$ teaspoon ground allspice
1 cup packed brown sugar	$1/4$ teaspoon ground cloves
1 teaspoon flour	$1/8$ teaspoon ground red pepper
1 cup cider vinegar	

Place the tomatoes and onions in a noncorrosive bowl, sprinkle with the salt, toss, and leave 6 to 8 hours or overnight. Next day, drain and rinse well with cold water.

Combine the tomatoes and onions with the sugar, flour, vinegar, mustard, celery seed, allspice, cloves, and red pepper in a saucepan. Bring to a boil, and simmer uncovered 25 to 30 minutes, until all is tender and the liquid is reduced but the mixture is still juicy. Can in sterile jars. Let sit a few days before serving. *Makes about 2 pints.*

GEORGIA PEACHES, PICKLED

*O*n Grandma's Christmas dinner table, among platters of turkey, corn bread dressing, giblet gravy, green beans, and other vegetables canned from summer's harvest, there always sat a big dish of pickled peaches. She hid several jars in a special hiding place in the fruit cellar for this occasion.

FIREPLACE RECIPE:

Take a gallon of clingstone peaches and peel as follows: plunge into boiling water and after a minute or two, drain and cover with cold water. Rub peeling off with a rag.

Put in kettle together with 2 pounds sugar and with this a pint and a little more of cider vinegar, boil to syrup. To this, put in 4 spoonfuls of whole cloves.

Boil syrup on slow coals a quarter of an hour and put peaches in, a few at a time so as to cover with juice. Simmer until tender, but no more. When easily pierced with broomstraw, put in jars or pack in stone crocks with covers well tied on. Boil syrup a few more minutes, then pour over peaches. Let season 3 days before using.

MODERN METHOD:

1 quart clingstone peaches	$1^1/4$ cups cider vinegar
$3/4$ cup granulated sugar	1 teaspoon whole cloves, or as desired*
$1/2$ cup firmly packed brown sugar	

Peel the peaches in a water bath as in the Fireplace Recipe above. In a separate 2-quart saucepan, prepare the syrup with sugar, vinegar, and cloves, and boil over medium heat 15 to 20 minutes to a heavy syrup. Place the peaches into the boiling syrup, as many at a time as can be covered, and cook over simmering heat about 10 to 12 minutes until just tender. Do not overcook. Test by inserting a toothpick.

Remove the peaches and place them in sterile pint jars. Boil the syrup 5 more minutes and pour over the peaches in the jars. Seal. Let season 3 days or more before using, 2 to 3 weeks for deeper flavor. *Makes 3 to 4 pints, depending on the size of the peaches.*

*For extra spicy flavor, stick an additional whole clove into each peach before boiling or canning.

134

GRAMMAR IN RHYME—FOR THE LITTLE FOLKS

It is seldom that one sees so much valuable matter as the following lines contain, comprised in so brief a space. Every young grammarian, and many older heads, will find it highly advantageous to commit the "poem" to memory; for with these lines at the tongue's end, none need ever mistake a part of speech:

1. Three little words you often see,
   Are articles—a, an, and the.

2. A Noun's the name of any thing,
   As school, or garden, hoop, or swing,

3. Adjectives tell the kind of Noun,
   As great, small, pretty, white, or brown.

4. Instead of Nouns the Pronouns stand—
   Her head, his face, your arm, my hand.

5. Verbs tell of something to be done—
   To read, count, sing, laugh, jump, or run.

6. How things are done, the adverbs tell,
   As slowly, quickly, ill, or well.

7. Conjunctions join the words together-
   As men and women, wind or weather.

8. The Preposition stands before
   A Noun, as in, or through a door.

9. The Interjection shows surprise,
   As oh! how pretty—ah! how wise.

The whole are called Nine Parts of Speech,
Which reading, writing, speaking, teach.

—From *Dr. Chase's Recipes* (1867)

WATERMELON RIND PICKLES

*G*randpa Ned made sure the hogs always got their share of watermelon rinds, but Grandma saw to it that there were always enough saved for her pickles.

FIREPLACE RECIPE:

Cut away peeling from a medium-size melon half and use only white portion of rind. Cut into thumb-size pieces and soak in brine till the morrow. Take out and wash good with fresh water, boil a few minutes then place in kettle with a pint vinegar and 2 pints sugar. Tie in spice bag a stick or two of cinnamon, 8 or 10 cloves, and a few slices of lemon. Drop into kettle and simmer all until rind is clear. Remove spice bag and pour syrup over rind in Mason jars and seal.

MODERN METHOD:

$1/2$ medium-size watermelon with thick rind	1 lemon, thinly sliced
$1/4$ cup salt in 1 quart water for brine	2 sticks cinnamon, broken in pieces
4 cups sugar	1 tablespoon whole cloves
2 cups cider vinegar diluted with $1/4$ cup water	

From the watermelon, pare the outside green skin and remove all the pink portions. Cut the white rind into 1-inch cubes or strips, measuring 4 cups.

Soak the rind overnight in the brine. Next day, drain and wash the rind thoroughly. Boil in fresh water 5 minutes. Drain.

Place the sugar and vinegar in a $2\frac{1}{2}$-quart pot. Tie the lemon, cinnamon sticks, and cloves in cheesecloth, drop the cloth into the pot, and bring to a boil. Add the rind.

Let simmer until the rind is tender and transparent, skimming occasionally if needed. Add a little water if necessary. Remove the spice bag and discard. Pack the rind in sterile jars. Heat the syrup to a rolling boil and pour over the rind. Seal while hot. Let sit a week before using. *Makes about 2 pints.*

⤜ SWEET PICKLED DRIED ⤛ PLUMS (PRUNES)

*G*randma often told of how she donned her bonnet and headed for the woods in late summer or early fall with a bucket to pick ripe, wild plums. Back home, she washed and split them to remove the pits and dried them in the sun, and they became Indian plums. This was a fun job except for sudden showers when she'd have to dash outside, rake the plums off the well cover into her apron skirt, and rush them inside out of the rain.

FIREPLACE RECIPE:

Take a half-gallon dried plums, cover with water, and let stand overnight to double. Cover and set pot on hot coals to one boil. Drain and set aside to prepare other.

In a kettle, put quarter amount of sugar as plums, half the vinegar as sugar, cloves, cinnamon, and ginger to taste. Bring to a good bubbling boil. To this put plums and simmer over low fire until tender and plums take most of the liquid.

Excellent accompaniment for chicken and dressing, or any meat.

Also spunks up greens.

MODERN METHOD:

4 cups pitted prunes, washed, cooked, and drained (1 pound raw)	4 whole cloves
1 cup sugar	1/2 teaspoon cinnamon
1/2 cup cider vinegar	1/4 teaspoon ginger

In a saucepan, cover the prunes with water, soak 24 hours, and then bring them to a boil in the same water. Remove from the heat at once, pour in a colander, and let drain.

In another saucepan, boil together the sugar, vinegar, and spices for 10 minutes. Add the drained prunes and simmer gently until very tender and most of the liquid has boiled out, being careful not to scorch the prunes. A spoonful of water may be added without affecting the flavor. Cool and use, or can in sterile jars while hot. You get a stronger flavor if the jars are sealed for at least 4 weeks. Good with both meats and vegetables. *Makes about 4 cups.*

⤜ PICKLED STRING BEANS ⤛

*G*randma religiously watched her planting and canning bible, the almanac. She would never plant seeds on the day the moon was new, saying the crop would be poor. She would never make pickles of any kind except when the moon was new, declaring that was the time they would be crispiest. These string beans proved her right.

FIREPLACE RECIPE:

On the new of the moon, pick a gallon of tender string beans, snip off the ends and string. Wash. Sprinkle with salt and leave in hot sun to dry 3 days. Wash.

Cover with water, then boil in kettle over low fire until tender. Drain off water and lay beans to dry. Pack upright as pencils into quart Mason jars.

Boil 2 quarts vinegar, a half-pound sugar, and a small handful of mixed, or favorite spices. Pour over beans and seal. Leave until the next new moon to open.

MODERN RECIPE:

2	quarts tender string beans	2 cups cider vinegar
4	tablespoons salt to 1 quart water for brine	1 cup sugar
		1 tablespoon mixed spices, if desired

Snip the ends, string, and wash the beans. Place in the brine and let remain 4 hours. Remove, drain, and wash. Cover with fresh water and boil until barely tender. Drain. Lay the beans singly on paper towels to dry, and then pack upright in quart canning jars, or pints if beans are short.

Boil the vinegar, sugar, and spices 5 or 6 minutes. While boiling hot, pour the vinegar over the beans in sterile jars and seal. Leave sealed a month. When opened, serve at room temperature, or place in the refrigerator and serve cold. Nice with hors d'oeuvres or as a snack. *Makes 4 pints.*

NOTE: Without spices, this dish has true bean flavor. Other spices, to taste, may be added to the vinegar before boiling. For milder flavor, substitute ¼ cup water for same of vinegar.

❧ PICKLED NASTURTIUMS ❧

*P*icklin' Pearl was a nickname my Great-Aunt Pearl acquired because she could pickle anything. Without ice to preserve nature's bounty, she learned the fine points of preserving with vinegar. You name it, she could pickle it. She mixed up this recipe on a dare.

FIREPLACE RECIPE:

Throw 2 or 3 handfuls small green nasturtium leaves into salt water. Leave 3 days. Drain. Same again. Pour off brine and cover with scalding vinegar having plenty dill seeds. Ready after a fortnight.

MODERN METHOD:

2 cups small, loosely packed, short-stemmed nasturtium leaves

6 tablespoons salt in 1 quart water for brine

1 cup cider vinegar

1 tablespoon dill seed

Cover the leaves with half the brine. Leave 3 days and drain. Cover the leaves with the other half of the brine and leave for 3 more days. Drain well. Place the leaves loosely in sterile jars. Pour the boiling vinegar with the dill seed over the leaves. Fill the jars and seal. Let sit 3 weeks for best flavor. *Makes about 2 cups.*

⤚ PICKLED CELERY ⤙

*P*icklin' Pearl had a never-ending stream of pickles for the family. She always tried to outdo her last one. This was one of the favorites.

FIREPLACE RECIPE:

There was no written recipe for these pickles.

MODERN METHOD:

3 stems white celery

6 tablespoons salt

1 quart water

1/4 cup (1/4-inch-thick) cucumber rounds

1 quart vinegar

1/4 cup brown sugar

1/4 teaspoon allspice

Trim and clean the celery stems. Break and pull off the strings. Cut in strips resembling long french fries the height of pint jars.

In a noncorrosive saucepan, place the salt and water, and bring to a boil to form a brine. Add the celery and cucumber rounds, and boil 8 to 10 minutes. Remove from the heat and drain. Discard the cucumber. Pack the celery strips upright in sterile pint jars.

In a saucepan, place the vinegar, sugar, and allspice, and bring to a good boil. Pour the hot mixture over the celery strips. Seal the jars. Let sit a month before using for the most delicious flavor. Good plain as finger food, or chopped in potato salad. *Makes about 2 pints.*

TO CLEAR HOUSES, BARNS E&C, OF RATS AND MICE

Gather the plant Dog's Tongue, the cynoglossum officinale of Linnaeus, which grows abundantly in every field; at the period when the sap is in its full vigor; bruise it with a hammer, or otherwise, and lay it in the house, barn or granary, infested by rats or mice, and those troublesome animals will immediately shift their quarters.

—From *Mackenzie's Five Thousand Receipts* (1852)

✂ PICKLED BLACKBERRIES ✂

his is another of Picklin' Pearl's gems. She claimed she almost didn't get to the house with enough berries to concoct this recipe. Said she was picking well toward the middle of the blackberry thicket when her foot felt a wiggle. She looked down and saw a blacksnake slithering away and dropped her bucket.

FIREPLACE RECIPE:

Make a syrup of sugar, vinegar, some spices as to liking in a kettle and place over low fire. When hot, put in usual bucket of berries and cook few minutes. Skim fruit into a gallon jar, cover with the syrup and turn a plate over it to keep berries below the surface. Can the berries while hot. Leave sealed 4 weeks for deeper flavor. No spices leaves deep berry flavor.

MODERN METHOD:

1½ cups sugar

1½ cups cider vinegar

4   cups ripe blackberries, washed and stemmed

1   teaspoon allspice*

Boil the sugar and vinegar 2 to 3 minutes to make a thin syrup. Add the berries and all-spice, and cook about 10 minutes, depending on the size of the berries. Remove all the scum as it arises. Can the berries with their juice in sterile jars while hot. Best when left sealed 3 to 4 weeks. *Makes about 2½ cups.*

*The allspice may be omitted to allow the true taste of the berries to come through.

SNAKE BITES

Make a stiff paste of the yolk of an egg and table salt. Apply at once.

—From *The Housekeeper Cook Book* (1894)

PICKLED STRAWBERRIES

*P*icklin' Pearl always had a delicacy for refreshments when the sewing circle met at her home. The favorite was these strawberries thinly sliced and placed on bakery bread rounds cut out with the lamp globe, spread thinly with fresh butter, then dusted with powdered sugar.

FIREPLACE METHOD:

Fill a jar with 6 quarts of berries not overripe. In boiler heat over slow fire 3 pints sugar and 1 pint vinegar. Pour over berries boiling hot and let stand a good day. Pour off the syrup, heat and return to fruit. Let stand until the morrow and boil all slowly till done. Keep in covered jars.

MODERN METHOD:

4	pints medium-size berries, not overripe	2	cups sugar
		1	cup cider vinegar

Place the berries in quart jars. In a saucepan, mix the sugar and vinegar, heat to boiling, and pour over the berries. The syrup should cover the berries. Let stand 24 hours.

Pour off the syrup, reheat it, and pour it over the fruit a second time. Let stand another 24 hours, and then cover and simmer slowly until tender. Do not overcook. Remove from the heat and individually place on a rack to dry. Cooking longer will mush the strawberries and result in pickled jam. Cover with the hot syrup, can in sterile jars, and put away 4 to 6 weeks for best flavor. *Makes about 6 cups.*

A NATURAL DENTIFRICE

The natural strawberry is a dentifrice, and its juice without any preparation, dissolves the tartareous incrustations on the teeth, and makes breath sweet and agreeable.

—From *Mackenzie's Five Thousand Receipts* (1852)

Desserts

☙ APPLE TORTEN CAKES ☙

*E*very fortnight, peddler Herbie, a carpetbagger turned Georgian, made a round through back roads in his old renovated hearse carrying merchandise of different kinds. It was known throughout the area as the traveling store. At Grandma's, she kept him sitting at the kitchen table eating treats until he emptied his mind of neighborhood gossip. Apple Torten Cakes were his favorite.

FIREPLACE RECIPE:

Make a dough with about a pint of flour having proper seasoning, a short tea-cup of sugar, several big spoons of fresh-churned butter, and a dash of nutmeg, and put to this 2 or 3 beaten eggs and several spoonfuls of left-over, strong coffee and enough milk for a stiff dough.

Roll dough very thin and spread over it some finely chopped apples, about a tea-cup, fold the dough over this, then roll it to sufficiently tighten apples. Cook as small cakes on bakestone until golden brown on both sides. Sprinkle with finest sugar while hot.

MODERN METHOD:

1 cup finely chopped cooking apples, about $^1/_2$ pound	$2^1/_2$ teaspoons baking powder
$^1/_2$ cup butter or margarine	$^3/_4$ teaspoon salt
$^3/_4$ cup sugar	$^1/_8$ teaspoon nutmeg
2 eggs, beaten	$^1/_3$ to $^1/_2$ cup milk
2 cups all-purpose flour	2 tablespoons cold strong coffee
	Confectioners' sugar to sprinkle

Preheat the oven to 350°. Peel, core, and grate the apples. In a large mixing bowl, cream the butter and sugar. Add the eggs and beat until smooth. Sift the flour, baking powder, salt, and nutmeg in another bowl, and gradually add, alternately, the milk mixed with the coffee. Combine thoroughly. Add a little more milk if necessary.

Roll out to $^1/_2$-inch thickness on a floured board, and spread the apples over half the dough. Fold the dough over the apples and smooth with a rolling pin. Cut the dough into 2-inch rounds with a biscuit cutter. Bake on a greased baking sheet for 20 to 25 minutes. Cover the tops with confectioners' sugar while hot. *Makes about 10 little cakes.*

❧ CHEROKEE LOAF CAKE ❧

*M*ama often said she loved the singsongy ca-chunk of the dasher hitting the clabber and cream in Grandma's big stone churn. Besides, clouds of fresh butter meant a goody like this loaf cake, a recipe handed down through generations by word of mouth from Grandma's Cherokee great-great-grandmother.

FIREPLACE RECIPE:

Warm ½ pound butter to a cream, and put in sugar, a coffee cup. Stir a few dozen rounds till quite light. Add a few dashes of ginger root scrapings and a little grated nutmeg. Work in 2 egg yolks. The whites of same must at this time be beaten to a strong snow, quite ready.

Sift flour, 2 coffee cups and a little more, and 2 or 3 hefty spoons cornmeal and a spoon of soda together. Add this and the milk and a cup of molasses to the whole, gently. Work in beaten egg whites.

Bake in a tin hoop or pan in Dutch oven over medium coals for 3 hours and put proper sheets of paper under it to keep it from burning.

MODERN METHOD:

2¼ cups all-purpose flour	½ cup sugar
½ cup cornmeal	2 egg yolks, beaten creamy
1 teaspoon baking soda	2 egg whites, beaten frothy
1 teaspoon ginger	1 cup cane molasses
⅛ teaspoon nutmeg	1 cup milk
½ cup butter or margarine	

Preheat the oven to 350°. Sift together the flour, cornmeal, baking soda, ginger, and nutmeg. In another bowl, cream the butter and sugar and blend in the egg yolks. Fold in the egg whites. In a large bowl, mix the molasses and milk, and add the flour mix alternately with the butter mixture. Combine well.

Bake in a 9 x 5-inch loaf pan 40 to 50 minutes, or until the sides shrink from the pan and a toothpick test comes out clean. This cake is especially good with Mahalia's Buttermilk Ice Cream (see page 185). *Makes 1 large loaf cake for about 8 servings.*

⮂ APPLE CIDER CAKE ⮀

*G*randma always began with a laugh when she told about Grandpa driving the wrong Model T pickup truck almost home from the trading post before he realized it wasn't his. He had loaded an identical truck with supplies, cranked it, and moseyed off. Just before reaching the lane to the house, he realized his mistake. Said he didn't mind the long drive back, the apologizing, or the reloading, but he hated having to wait to eat his favorite Apple Cider Cake, which Grandma had ready for his birthday.

FIREPLACE RECIPE:

Beat a half dozen or so eggs together with a mold of butter and 3 tea-cups sugar. Stir in a scant quart of flour, then a short pint of apple cider with a little lemon juice. Bake in Dutch oven layered with parchment.

When done, spread layers and top with cider filling. Mix cider with lemon juice to a cup, half that plus a little more of sugar, a dash of salt, and thickening flour. Cook till thick as desired. Mix in a walnut size lump of fresh-churned butter. Cool and spread.

MODERN METHOD:

1^1/$_4$ cups sugar	^{1}/$_4$ teaspoon salt
^{1}/$_2$ cup butter or margarine	1 cup less 1 tablespoon apple cider
3 eggs, well beaten	1 tablespoon lemon juice
2^1/$_2$ cups all-purpose flour	Apple Cider Filling (recipe follows)
2^1/$_2$ teaspoons baking powder	

Preheat the oven to 350°. Cream the sugar and butter and add the eggs. In another bowl, sift together the flour, baking powder, and salt. Add the dry ingredients to the butter mixture, alternating with a blend of the cider and lemon juice. Mix well.

Pour the batter into three greased, round 9-inch cake pans, and bake for 25 to 30 minutes, or until a toothpick inserted in the center comes out clean. Cool on a rack. Spread the Apple Cider Filling between the layers and on the top. *Makes 1 three-layer cake for 10 servings.*

Apple Cider Filling

1	tablespoon flour	1	tablespoon lemon juice
2	tablespoons cornstarch	1	cup apple cider (scant)
$^2/_3$	cup sugar	2	tablespoons butter or margarine
$^1/_2$	teaspoon salt		

Mix the flour, cornstarch, sugar, and salt in the top of a double boiler. Stir in the lemon juice and cider. Mix until smooth. Cook over boiling water to the desired thickness, stirring constantly. Add the butter. Cool and spread the filling on the cake.

RHEUMATISM, NEW REMEDY

Kerosene oil 3 ozs; skunk's oil 1 oz; mix, and shake when applied. Put it on quite freely, and heat it in the stove, or by means of a hot shovel. One of our physicians in this city has used a preparation very nearly resembling the above but varying sufficient to satisfy myself that any other animal oil will do as well as that from the highly-flavored one above mentioned. He used kerosene oil 2 oz.; neats-foot oil 1 oz.; oil of origanum $^1/_2$ oz.; mixed and shaken as used. The smell of the kerosene is not very pleasant, but if a pair of ankles and feet, badly swollen, so much so that you could not walk on them for months, could be cured in two or three weeks, as it was in this case, it might be well to put up with its disagreeable smell. Rub and heat it in thoroughly twice daily.

—From *Dr. Chase's Recipes* (1867)

∽ SKILLET PEANUT TEA CAKE ∽

I can still see Grandma hunkered down in front of the fireplace with the bill of her bonnet pulled well forward. She removed a black iron skillet from the trivet with both hands padded with big quilted pot holders and set it on a little square board on the cook table. When a chunk of butter she placed on top of the cake ran down the sides, she cut me a big wedge right out of the skillet.

FIREPLACE RECIPE:

Place in iron skillet a little fresh butter and melt. In proper bowl, lay a half-pint fresh-parched peanuts pounded to half. Now add a half-pint of mixed white and brown sugar and a little milk. Beat 4 eggs colorless and add, then ½ pint flour with proper saleratus* and salt.

When the whole is mixed, pour in skillet, cover and bake over low coals until broom straw stuck to center comes clean. Drop a dollop of butter on top. A good accompaniment for coffee or tea.

MODERN METHOD:

2 tablespoons butter plus extra for brushing	4 eggs, beaten
¹/₂ cup granulated sugar	¹/₄ cup milk
¹/₂ cup packed brown sugar	1 cup all-purpose flour
¹/₂ cup chunky-style peanut butter	1 teaspoon baking powder
	¹/₈ teaspoon salt

Preheat the oven to 350°. Melt the butter in heavy, 8-inch, ovenproof skillet. In a mixing bowl, combine the granulated and brown sugars. Add the peanut butter, eggs, and milk and mix well. Sift the flour, baking powder, and salt together, and stir into the peanut butter mixture a little at a time until smooth.

Pour the batter into the skillet. Cover with an ovenproof lid, or foil, and bake about 45 minutes, or until a knife inserted in the center comes out clean. Brush the top with butter, let stand a few minutes, and serve. *Makes 6 servings.*

NOTE: This is a good tea cake or between-meal snack.

*Baking soda.

⤜ PORK CAKE ⤛

(without butter, milk, or eggs)

*C*ousin Girdie Mae was one determined lady. When her cow went dry and eggs became scarce after she fried most of her pullets, she satisfied her hankering for cake with this recipe.

FIREPLACE RECIPE:

Take fat, salt pork, entirely free of lean or rind, chopped so fine as to be almost like lard 1 short lb.: pour boiling water upon it about ½ pint; raisins seeded and chopped 1 lb.; a few currants, citron shaved into shreds ¼ lb.; sugar about a pint; molasses near ½ pint; saleratus* 1 tea-spoon, rubbed fine and put into the molasses.

Mix all together and stir in flour as common cake mixtures, then stir in nutmeg and cloves finely ground 1 oz. each; cinnamon, also fine, 2 ozs. Place on 10 layers of paper in spider pan on low coals. When nothing adheres it is done. It should be baked slowly.

You can substitute other fruit in place of the raisins, if desired, using as much or as little as you please, or none at all, and still have a nice cake. It is still nice weeks after it is baked.

MODERN METHOD:

½	cup lard	½	teaspoon salt
½	cup boiling water	1	tablespoon nutmeg
1	cup sugar	¾	tablespoon cloves
½	teaspoon baking soda	2	tablespoons cinnamon
½	cup dark molasses	1	cup raisins, chopped
2¾	cups all-purpose flour	¼	cup currants
2	teaspoons baking powder	¼	cup citron, slivered

Preheat the oven to 325°. Combine the lard, boiling water, and sugar in a saucepan. Mix the baking soda with the molasses and pour this into the lard mixture.

In a large bowl, sift together the flour, baking powder, salt, nutmeg, cloves, and cinnamon. Mix in the raisins, currants, and citron. Gradually blend the dry ingredients into the lard mixture.

Bake in a lightly greased and floured 9 x 5-inch loaf pan for 1 hour and 15 minutes, or until a toothpick inserted comes out clean. Stays good several weeks. *Makes 1 large loaf cake for 12 servings.*

VARIATION: Chopped nuts may be added with raisins.

*Baking soda.

GREAT-GRANDMA RACHEL'S GINGER PLANKS

*G*randma often commented that she made these cookies just to see her grandchildren's eyes widen at the story that went with them. As the kids nibbled, she told her age-old tale about when she was little and saw her papa get shot in the leg with an Indian's arrow. When they stopped under a shade tree to remove the arrow, a group of Indians swamped them, apologizing for shooting at the wrong wagon. To keep Grandma and her siblings from getting too excited, her ma kept them eating ginger planks till the Indians removed the arrow and cauterized the wound with ground black pepper.

FIREPLACE RECIPE:

Take a pint of molasses, mix in a quarter-pint sugar and a half-pint butter. Put to this a big spoon of ground cinnamon, a little ginger, a pinch of salt, and a spoon of soda. Pour over all a quarter-pint of boiling water and stir well. Mix in flour to a stiff dough and mold into fairly thin planks rounded on the ends. Bake slow in spider over slow coals. Easy to burn. Keeps good for a fortnight in a tight box.

MODERN METHOD:

$^1/_4$ cup sugar	$^1/_4$ cup boiling water
$^3/_4$ teaspoon ground cinnamon	$^1/_2$ cup butter or margarine
$^3/_4$ teaspoon ground ginger	1 cup sugarcane molasses
$^1/_2$ teaspoon salt	$2^1/_2$ cups all-purpose flour
1 teaspoon baking soda	

Preheat the oven to 275°. In a bowl, sift the sugar, cinnamon, ginger, salt, and baking soda. Combine the boiling water, butter, and molasses. Add the molasses to the sugar mix slowly, mixing well. Let cool slightly and blend in the flour to make a stiff dough.

Roll out the dough on a floured board to $^1/_2$ inch thick. With a sharp knife, cut strips about 2 inches wide and 4 inches long. Round out each end with a floured knife. Place on a greased cookie sheet 2 inches apart.

Bake in the oven, watching carefully since the strips burn easily. Remove when slightly brown. The cookies stay fresh for 2 weeks or more in a closed container. *Makes about 10 planks.*

GRANDMA'S GINGERSNAPS

*M*ama said when she was a tot, she often sang "Southern Baby's First Song" to Grandma. Before she finished the "Yes Ma'am, No Ma'am, Thank you Ma'am, Please," Grandma would smile and set the big square, gallon cookie jar on the table, reach in, and hand her a cookie. Mama said that before biting into it, she would trace the deep cracks on top with her finger, believing they would lead her to fairyland.

FIREPLACE RECIPE:

Mix well together a pint of finest flour, two little spoonfuls of baking soda, 2 pinches of salt, a little spoonful of ginger.

In another bowl, mix together a half-pound of lard, less 2 or 3 spoonfuls, and a half pint sugar, and stir into this a quarter pint of molasses and a fresh egg, whipped. Put all together with flour mixture to make dough.

Put in cool place to get cold. Shape dough into walnut-size balls and when they are spread out in the right form on pie tin, flatten and sprinkle with sugar and cook in a brisk Dutch oven until snappish.

MODERN METHOD:

$^3/_4$ cup shortening	2 cups all-purpose flour
$^3/_4$ cup sugar plus $^1/_4$ cup for sprinkling	2 teaspoons baking soda
$^1/_2$ cup molasses	$^1/_4$ teaspoon salt
1 egg, beaten	$1^1/_4$ teaspoons ginger

Cream together the shortening and $^3/_4$ cup sugar, and add the molasses and egg. Sift the flour with the soda, salt, and ginger, and gradually stir this into the creamed mixture a little at a time, mixing thoroughly after each addition. Chill in the refrigerator.

Preheat the oven to 375°. Remove the dough and shape it into small balls, about 1 inch in diameter. Place the balls on a greased baking sheet and flatten to $^1/_4$-inch thickness with the bottom of a glass. Sprinkle the tops with the remaining $^1/_4$ cup sugar. Bake in the oven 12 to15 minutes, or until lightly browned. Remove the gingersnaps and cool on racks. *Makes about 2 dozen gingersnaps.*

OATMEAL LOGS

*G*randpa's coon dogs chased a pack of field rats up the water well's square, waist-high, wood frame when the top was open, and the rats plunged down into the water, polluting it. After a few weeks of bringing water from the spring, Grandma was so glad to get a well at the house that she kept the dowser snacking on Oatmeal Logs while he located water with his diving rod and dug the new well.

FIREPLACE RECIPE:

Put together a pint and a half of the best flour and appropriate salt and rising powder. To this put a little sugar. Scald a half-pint and a spoon or two of fresh milk, mix in a few blades* of honey, and pour over a half tea-cup of rolled oats, then mix into the whole.

Now put in a walnut-size lump of soft lard. Cool and work with hands till smooth. Roll into sticks about the thickness and half the length of a lead pencil, or as choose. Bake in a rather hot Dutch oven or spider pan till done, then roll in best grade of white or brown sugar.

MODERN METHOD:

3 cups all-purpose flour
$1/2$ teaspoon salt
1 tablespoon sugar
2 teaspoons baking powder
$1^1/4$ cups scalded milk

1 tablespoon honey
$1/2$ cup old-fashioned oatmeal
$1/4$ cup butter or margarine, melted
Sugar, granulated or brown, for sprinkling

In a mixing bowl, sift together the flour, salt, sugar, and baking powder. In a double boiler, scald the milk, blend in the honey, mix thoroughly, and pour over the oatmeal. Add the butter. Cool. Add to the sifted ingredients and mix until smooth.

Preheat the oven to 375°. Roll out the dough on a lightly floured board to about $1/4$-inch thickness, and cut strips 3 to 4 inches long, or shorter if desired. Bake in the oven about 8 to 10 minutes. Sprinkle or roll in sugar as desired. *Makes about 15 (4-inch) logs.*

*A measure on a knife, about $1/2$ teaspoon.

☙ OATEN SNACK CAKES ❧

*G*randma often told about the day she and Grandpa went to town with their five hundred dollars and purchased their Model T Ford touring car. Grandpa drove the car home after a driving lesson, while she followed in the buggy. Without much time to prepare supper, she toasted Oaten Snack Cakes made the day before, and served them with chicken-fried salt meat, scrambled eggs, and grits with Sawmill Gravy (see page 102).

FIREPLACE RECIPE:

Crumble a bit of butter about the size of a small egg into a quart of oatmeal with a heavy pinch of salt and enough warm water to make a moderately stiff paste. Pat it in the hands with plenty oatmeal strewn under and over it. Roll it out as thin as can be made. The cakes should be prepared singly and baked on a girdle iron,* turned while they are doing, and afterwards toasted a little before the fire to render them crisp.

They must always be kept very dry.

Oaten-cakes may be baked in small sizes a few minutes in a Dutch oven instead of a girdle iron when but heated on moderately hot coals.

MODERN METHOD:

4 cups old-fashioned oatmeal	3 tablespoons butter or margarine, melted
1/4 teaspoon salt	Extra oatmeal for rolling

Preheat the oven to 400°. Combine the oatmeal, salt, and butter in a mixing bowl. Add enough warm water to make a very stiff dough.

Turn the dough out onto a board sprinkled with oatmeal, and roll out very thin. Cut into cakes with a biscuit cutter. Place on a lightly greased cookie sheet with a spatula, and bake in the oven 6 to 8 minutes until the cakes begin to brown. Do not allow them to get fully brown.

Cool, then toast lightly in a cool oven to crisp just before serving. Delicious topped with jelly or jam. *Makes 10 snack cakes.*

*Griddle.

⌘ FRIED MILK PATTIES ⌘

*C*ousin Addie Belle was quite well-to-do, but she had the reputation of being so stingy that she squeezed a penny until you could hear Lincoln squeal a mile away. This is one of her low-cost goodies.

FIREPLACE RECIPE:

Take a pint of fresh milk, mostly cream, put in saucepan with a stick of cinnamon. To it put thickening flour, less than pint sugar, few vanilla beans, and yolks of 3 eggs well beat. Set pan on trivet over slow coals, stir briskly till thick, and take away. Discard cinnamon stick and beans, stir in a dollop of butter, and pour thin layer of mix onto greased platter. Leave until cold and stiff, then let same be cut into strips size of finger. Gently coat with fine biscuit crumbs, then in sweetened egg whipped; then roll again in crumbs. Fry quick in boiling lard till properly colored.

MODERN METHOD:

2 tablespoons cornstarch	$^1/_4$ teaspoon cinnamon
2 tablespoons flour	$^1/_2$ teaspoon vanilla extract
$^1/_4$ teaspoon salt	$^1/_2$ cup toasted breadcrumbs,
$^1/_3$ to $^1/_2$ cup sugar, or to taste	crushed, or cracker meal, for coating
1 cup milk	1 egg beaten with1 teaspoon sugar
1 cup cream	Oil for frying
3 egg yolks, beaten	
1 tablespoon butter or margarine	

In the top of a double boiler, combine the cornstarch, flour, salt, and sugar. Mix the milk and cream, and add gradually to the flour mix, stirring until smooth. Place the top of the double boiler over simmering water, stirring constantly.

Place the egg yolks in a separate small container, such as a cup. When the mixture begins to thicken, dribble about $^1/_2$ cup of the hot liquid into the eggs while stirring briskly and return the eggs to the mix. Cook and stir until the mix coats the spoon and remove from the heat. Blend in the butter, cinnamon, and vanilla. Pour the mix $^1/_2$ inch deep on a lightly greased platter. Chill in the refrigerator. When cold, the mix will be fairly stiff.

With a thin, sharp knife, cut into strips about ½ inch wide and 2 to 3 inches long. Handling carefully, roll each strip in the dry breadcrumbs, then in the sweetened egg mix, and then again in the crumbs. Place in the refrigerator a second time, chill, and then dip individually into a skillet of hot oil briefly until light brown. Remove from the oil.

Preheat the oven to 350°. Arrange the strips on a greased cookie sheet, and place in the oven 4 or 5 minutes to warm through and through. Serve warm. *Makes about 15 patties.*

VARIATION: Add ground nuts to the egg coating before frying.

TOBACCO SUBSTITUTE*

Buck bean is very common in shallow ponds; and is distinguishable by its leaves growing in threes, and its pink and white flowers being shaggy on their inner surface. By some persons the leaves of buck bean are smoked instead of tobacco; and different preparations of this plant have been found efficacious as a remedy against agues,† and in rheumatisms and dropsy.

There is an opinion that sheep, when compelled to eat of buck bean, are cured of the rot. In Lapland, it is said that the pounded roots, though very unpalatable, are sometimes converted into bread.

—From *Useful Knowledge* by Reverend William Bingley (1818)

*Handwritten note at this location: "Never chew dried sweet flag root. Will quell desire for tobacco cigarettes."

†Chills and fever.

MAUDIE'S RECEPTION COOKIES

The day Aunt Maudie's daughter was left waiting at the church by a traveling salesman, Grandma had carried a batch of these cookies to the church to add to the reception goodies. After the marrying collapsed, folks still partied, glad the salesman was traveling elsewhere.

FIREPLACE RECIPE:

Sift sugar, one and a half pounds, a little pounded cinnamon, and nutmeg grated, into six tea-cups flour with rising. Add a little cream to about a half-dozen eggs well-frothed. Mix them with the flour, add grated rind and juice of two large lemons, then pour as much soft butter as will make it a good thick paste to roll out into very thin cakes, about a tea-cup and a half. Cut out with lamp globe bottom. Bake them in a quick Dutch oven after sprinkling joined finger-size rings of sugar on the tops carefully with a little spoon.

MODERN METHOD:

^{1}/$_2$ cup butter or margarine	2 teaspoons baking powder
1 cup sugar plus sugar for tops	^{1}/$_4$ teaspoon salt
2 eggs, beaten	^{1}/$_4$ teaspoon cinnamon
^{1}/$_4$ cup half-and-half	^{1}/$_4$ teaspoon nutmeg
1 teaspoon grated lemon rind	2 cups all-purpose flour
2 tablespoons lemon juice	

Preheat the oven to 350°. Warm the butter slightly and cream with the 1 cup sugar. Beat until light and fluffy. Gradually beat in the egg, half-and-half, lemon rind, and lemon juice. Sift the baking powder, salt, cinnamon, and nutmeg with the flour, and add to the sugar mixture a little at a time to make a soft dough. Knead.

On a floured board, roll the dough to 1/4-inch thickness, and cut rounds with a biscuit cutter. With a small spoon or cookie spreader, gently sprinkle the tops with the extra sugar in a pattern forming an interlocked, finger-size set of rings.

Place on a greased cookie sheet, and bake in the oven 8 to 10 minutes or until golden brown. *Makes about 3 dozen cookies.*

∽ FLAKY PASTE ∽

*O*ne of Great-Grandma's "receipts" that Grandma learned to make and call her staple was this crust. She loved it best filled with beefsteak stew, but also made it often for vegetable pies and dessert custards with meringue.

FIREPLACE RECIPE:

Sift a pint of flour and proper salt into a bowl. Chop in a half-pint butter or lard or mixture of same with a knife till well mixed. Add cold water to form a dough, mixing paste thoroughly while adding water.

Flour a board and roll the paste out very thin, rolling only lengthwise, and keeping the edges straight; then fold evenly into three layers lengthwise, turn it half around and roll again.

Repeat the folding and rolling twice and chill the paste if possible before baking. It is the folding and rolling that produce the flakes. Will make crust and a cover.

For beefsteak stew, a little hole may be cut in top crust after pie is ready, and a little boiling water poured in to form additional gravy.

MODERN METHOD:

2 cups sifted all-purpose flour	1 cup shortening
1/2 teaspoon salt	6 tablespoons ice water

Preheat the oven to 450°. Sift the flour and salt together and cut in the shortening. Add a tablespoon of water at a time, using enough to make a dough without its being crumbly.

Roll out the dough very thin, and fold it evenly in three layers lengthwise like a sheet of paper is folded to fit in an envelope. Turn it half around and roll again. Repeat the folding and rolling twice. It is the folding and rolling that produce the flakes.

For two single crusts, divide the dough in half and roll each piece out to 1/8-inch thickness to fit the pie plates. If the crusts are for a precooked filling, chill before baking. Prick the bottoms with a fork five or six times. Bake in the oven 12 to 15 minutes until golden tan.

If a top crust is desired for a pie with a prebaked filling, roll out the other half of the dough to cover the filling. Or cut the dough into strips, bake separately, and top the pie, crisscross or as desired.

The crust may be baked along with the filling, according to the filling directions. *Makes 2 single-crust pastries or 1 double-crust pastry.*

⁓ PUFF PASTE POCKETS ⁓

*G*randma demanded that her daughters learn to cook unassisted by their tenth birthday. My mama declared if Grandma said it once, she said it a hundred times: "Good, attractive food will turn a man into a beau." This is one of the recipes they learned early on.

FIREPLACE RECIPE:

Make paste day before used. Beat one fresh egg yolk and add it to a good $\frac{1}{4}$ tea-cup of water and a little lemon juice. Sift a pint of good flour, proper salt. Mix to firm dough. Roll out onto oblong sheet.

Wash fresh-churned butter and press into a flat cake half as large as the dough, lay on one end, and flop dough over it. Press edges well together, roll and fold in three layers. Cool. Put outside to chill if winter.

Roll again, repeating till the paste has been rolled seven times. Butter may be divided into three portions and put in after each rolling, but the seven rollings must be made after all the butter has been used. Roll paste very thin and cut into rounds size of lamp globe bottom. With a cutter or top of medicine glass several sizes smaller, remove centers from half the portions first cut, discard centers; place rings thus formed on the whole rounds of paste. Chill before baking a few at a time in covered spider pan on medium hearth coals. Best use trivet.

When cool, fill centers with jelly or jam, or leave plain.

MODERN METHOD:

1 egg yolk, beaten	2 cups all-purpose flour
4 to 5 tablespoons ice water	$\frac{1}{2}$ teaspoon salt
1 teaspoon lemon juice	$\frac{1}{2}$ cup butter or margarine, softened

Mix the beaten egg yolk with the ice water, add the lemon juice, and beat until smooth. Sift together the flour and salt. Add to the egg mixture a little at a time to form a firm dough.

On a floured board, roll the dough into an oblong sheet, and spread the softened butter on half the dough at one end. Fold the dough over the buttered side like a big tart. Press the edges together, roll out, and fold into three layers. Chill 30 minutes. Repeat the folding and rolling seven times after the butter is used.

Preheat the oven to 450°. Roll the dough to slightly less than ¼-inch thickness and cut it into 3-inch rounds. With a cutter several sizes smaller, cut, remove, and discard the centers from half of the 3-inch rounds. Place the rounds with a hole over the larger rounds. Press the edges firmly together, making a pocket. Bake in the oven 15 to 18 minutes until golden brown. Fill the pockets (the cut-out centers) with your favorite jelly or jam. *Makes 8 pockets.*

CINNAMON

Cinnamon is the under bark of the branches of a tree of the bay tribe. Cinnamon is examined and arranged according to its quality by persons, who, for this purpose, are obliged to taste and chew it. This is a very troublesome and disagreeable office; few persons being able to hold out more than two or three days successively, as the cinnamon deprives the tongue and lips of all the mucus with which they are covered.

The virtues of cinnamon . . . are not confined to the bark. The *leaves,* the *fruit,* and the *root,* all yield oil of considerable value. That from fruit is highly fragrant, of thick consistence, and at Ceylon was formerly made into candles for the sole use of the king.

—From *Useful Knowledge* by Reverend William Bingley (1818)

PASTRY GLAZE

*G*randma cooked not only for taste but for beauty. Her familiar phrase was, "If it's pretty outside, your taster sees and
remembers, even if the inside is less than good."

FIREPLACE RECIPE:

To prevent juice from sogging bottom pie crust, beat an egg well, and with a bit of
cloth, wet the crust of the pie with the beaten egg just before you put in the pie mixture.

For pies which have a top crust also, wet the top with the same before baking,
which gives it a beautiful shiny brown. It gives beauty also to biscuit, ginger cakes, and
other flour bakings.

MODERN METHOD:

The same basic recipe is used today.

⤥ GRANDMA'S MOLASSES PIE ⤦

*C*ooking this pie reminded Grandma to tell her friends not to drink sugarcane juice while it's being cooked to molasses in the big vat over a pine-knot fire. She would never forget that after drinking two cups, she was sick for three days.

FIREPLACE RECIPE:

Mix together a pint molasses, little thickening flour, little sugar, pinch of nutmeg, dollop of butter, 3 eggs beaten to 1 color, teaspoon soda. Pour in crust glazed with egg.

MODERN METHOD:

$^1/_2$ recipe Flaky Paste (see page 157)

3 eggs, beaten (use 1 teaspoon for glaze)

2 cups cane molasses

2 tablespoons cornstarch

1 teaspoon baking soda

1 tablespoon butter

$^1/_2$ teaspoon nutmeg

Make a single-crust pie shell, using the Flaky Paste recipe. Glaze the bottom with the 1 teaspoon beaten egg.

Preheat the oven to 325°. Mix together the 3 eggs, molasses, cornstarch, baking soda, butter, and nutmeg and beat well. Pour into the raw crust. Bake 30 to 40 minutes in the oven until a toothpick inserted in the center comes out clean. Remove from the oven and cool on a rack. *Makes 6 servings.*

❧ BUTTERMILK PUDDIN' PIE ❧

In Grandma's day, it was a sin to turn a hand to any kind of work on the Sabbath, so she cooked enough food on Saturday to last until Monday. This was one of her staples.

FIREPLACE RECIPE:

Crust. Put ½ pint flour, same cornmeal, rising, lump of lard, dash of salt, a little sugar and work together. Put fresh milk for firm dough. Fit in pie pan. Bake with filling: Take yolks of several fresh-laid eggs, beat-up well. To this put a short pint of sugar, thickening flour, egg-size lump of sweet butter melted. To the whole, mix in a pint of fresh-churned buttermilk. Mix in egg whites whipped stiff. Drop in few vanilla beans but remove. Pour in crust, sprinkle with a little grated nutmeg and bake.

MODERN METHOD:

Cornmeal Pastry

1 cup cornmeal	2½ tablespoons sugar
1 cup all-purpose flour	½ cup butter or margarine
2 teaspoons baking powder	½ cup milk
½ teaspoon salt	

Sift together the cornmeal, flour, baking powder, salt, and sugar. Cut in the butter to a pea-size consistency. Mix with the milk to make a firm dough. Cover and chill. On a floured board, roll out the dough thicker than normal, about ¼ inch. Fit into a 9-inch pie pan.

Filling and Assembly

¼ cup butter or margarine	2 tablespoons cornstarch
1 cup sugar	1½ cups buttermilk
4 egg yolks beaten, save whites	4 egg whites, frothed
1 teaspoon vanilla	⅛ teaspoon nutmeg, for sprinkling
1 tablespoon flour	

Preheat the oven to 425°. Cream the butter and sugar and add the egg yolks and vanilla. Mix together the flour and cornstarch and blend alternately with the buttermilk. Stir until smooth and fold in the well-beaten egg whites.

Pour the mixture into the crust. Sprinkle the top with the nutmeg. Bake in the oven 10 minutes. Reduce the temperature to 325°, and bake 20 to 25 minutes or until a knife inserted in the center comes out clean. Remove from the oven. Cool on a rack. *Makes 6 servings.*

VARIATION: For a cheesecake, add 1 teaspoon grated lemon rind and 1 tablespoon lemon juice to the batter mix. Before baking, sprinkle the top lightly with additional nutmeg.

THE FIG

The fruit is on short and thick stalks, of purplish colour, and contains a soft, sweet and fragrant pulp intermixed with numerous small seeds. Figs are dried either by furnace, or in the sun, after having been dipped in a scalding hot ley made of the ashes of the fig-tree. In this state they are used both in medicine and as food; and are considered more wholesome and more easy of digestion than when fresh.

The wood of the fig tree . . . is almost indestructible, and on this account, was formerly employed in eastern countries for the preservation of embalmed bodies.

—From *Useful Knowledge* by Reverend William Bingley (1818)

↭ HATTIE'S VINEGAR CAKE-PIE ↭

*G*randma's sister Hattie was proud of her upstairs balcony. It overlooked the pond in the green horse pasture where she hid her silver tableware when the Yankees marched through Atlanta during the Civil War. Aunt Hattie always served dessert to guests on this balcony using her "educated" silverware, especially with this pie, which was a regular.

FIREPLACE RECIPE:

In overly deep pie plate, make a pastry crust; lightly coat bottom with butter and bake to harden. Let wait. In saucepan, mix $1\frac{1}{2}$ pts. water, $\frac{1}{2}$ pt. molasses, same of vinegar, same of flour, same of sugar, pinch salt and a little lemon juice. Set over fire and stir. When a little thick, take up and add dollop of butter. Pour in prepared pastry. Bake.

MODERN METHOD:

$\frac{1}{2}$ recipe Flaky Paste (see page 157)
1 cup all-purpose flour
1 cup sugar
$\frac{1}{2}$ teaspoon salt
3 cups water

1 cup molasses (prefer sugarcane)
1 cup vinegar
$\frac{1}{2}$ teaspoon lemon juice
2 teaspoons butter or margarine, melted
Meringue (recipe follows)

Preheat the oven to 450°. Make a single-crust pie shell in a pie plate at least 1 inch deep, using the Flaky Paste recipe. Prick with a fork. Partially bake for 7 to 10 minutes to harden and avoid sogginess.

In a double boiler, mix the flour, sugar, and salt. Add the water a little at a time. Beat until smooth. Blend in the molasses, vinegar, lemon juice, and butter. Set the mixture over boiling water. Stir constantly till slightly thickened. Remove.

Pour the mixture into the pastry shell. Reduce the oven to 350° and bake about 30 minutes, or until a toothpick inserted in the center comes out clean. Spoon the meringue over the filling, reduce the oven to 325°, and bake until the peaks are golden, 10 to 15 minutes. *Makes 8 servings.*

Meringue

1/4 teaspoon cream of tartar

1/4 teaspoon salt

3 egg whites

3 tablespoons sugar

Add the cream of tartar and salt to the egg whites and beat until frothy. Add the sugar gradually, beating well after each addition. Beat until peaks form when the beater is lifted. Spoon over the pie filling and bake according to the recipe.

THE SWEET-SCENTED VIOLET

The sweet-scented violet is cultivated in large quantity. The *petals* of which are used for giving colour to *syrup of violets;* an officinal preparation of which is kept in the shops, and is given as an agreeable laxative to children.

This syrup is also employed, in chemical inquiries, for discovering the presence of acids and alkalis. The *seeds,* and the *roots,* in a powdered state, were formerly used in medicine.

—From *Useful Knowledge* by Reverend William Bingley (1818)

❧ TUTTI-FRUITTI TARTS ❧

*C*ousin Viola was worried that her twenty-eight-year-old bachelor son would never marry, but he finally found a girl he liked. She was undignified with her drugstore orange hair, and bobbed to boot, fire engine red lips, jet-black eyebrows, skinny-as-grasshopper legs, and knee-showing dresses. Even so, Viola was so proud, she made these snacks for their Sunday afternoon sparkings at the springhouse.

FIREPLACE RECIPE:

Take a pound of dough made for white bread, roll it out and put dollops* of butter upon same till a pound has been worked in. Roll out very thin, then cut it into squares twice the size the tarts are wanted.

Prepare filling with a handful of raisins, same of dried figs and finely cut pecans. To this put a little lemon juice, a little rind grated, some unrefined sugar or melted molasses sugar or brown sugar, a dash of flour to thicken, and two or three eggs beaten together. Set pot on low fire, simmer and stir a good half-hour until no liquid runs. Remove from fire.

Put a bit of filling upon each square of paste, close it tight in Dutch Oven and lay tarts separate to bake moderately, a few at a time with embers in lid. Afterwards, when taken out, sift sugar over them.

MODERN METHOD:

Filling

$^1/_2$ cup chopped raisins	1 egg, beaten
$^1/_4$ cup chopped dried figs	1 teaspoon grated lemon rind
$^1/_2$ cup chopped pecans	1 tablespoon lemon juice
1 teaspoon cornstarch	$^3/_4$ cup brown sugar
2 teaspoons flour	1 tablespoon dark molasses
2 tablespoons water	

Make the filling first so it can cool while you make the pastry. Mix the raisins, figs, pecans, cornstarch, flour, water, egg, lemon rind and juice, sugar, and molasses, and simmer over low heat 8 to 10 minutes, stirring constantly. Remove from the heat and let cool.

Pastry and Assembly

2 cups all-purpose flour, sifted	$^1/_4$ cup cold water
1 teaspoon salt	Milk for brushing
$^3/_4$ cup shortening	Sugar for sprinkling

Preheat the oven to 425°. Sift together the flour and salt in a mixing bowl. Cut in the shortening until the mixture is the consistency of small peas. Sprinkle with the cold water until the dough holds together when balled.

Roll to $^1/_4$-inch thickness and cut into 3- to 4-inch squares. Place a rounded tablespoon of the filling on each square and fold over to make a three-cornered tart. If making smaller or larger tarts, adjust the filling. Wet your fingers to pinch the edges together. Brush the tops lightly with milk, sprinkle sparsely with the sugar, and prick with a fork.

Place on greased baking tins. Bake in the oven 10 to 12 minutes or until brown. *Makes 8 to 10 tarts*.

CURE FOR CORNS

If a cripple will take a lemon, cut off a piece, then nick it so as to let in the toe with the corn, the pulp next the corn—tie this on at night, so that it cannot move—he will find next morning that, with a blunt knife, the corn will come away to a great extent. Two or three applications of this will make a "poor cripple" happy for life. —*London Field*.

—From *Dr. Chase's Recipes* (1867)

⤙ COUNTRY CHEESE PIE ⤚

*G*randma often told about how she learned to cook her mother's and grandmother's recipes. She complained that she was about nine before she got this one just right.

FIREPLACE RECIPE:

Place a quart of clabber in drip bag overnight. When clabber is dry, measure out a tea-cup full, put in patty pan and mash crumbly with a fork. To this, add a half tea-cup of sweet cream, a short tea-cup of sugar and a little thickening flour and a pinch of salt. Place mix in a patty-pan in the Dutch oven having finger-width of water and settle oven on trivet over medium coals. Stir until a little thick.

Remove oven from coals, cool mix slightly, beat in two or three egg yolks, return to heat and cook till about pudding-thick. Add juice and rind of a lemon and cook a little more. Pour into baked pie pastry.

Cover with egg-white meringue and bake.

MODERN METHOD:

1/2 recipe Flaky Paste (see page 157)	3 egg yolks, save whites
1 cup small-curd cottage cheese, drained	2 tablespoons lemon juice
1/2 cup half-and-half	1/2 teaspoon grated lemon rind
3/4 cup sugar	Meringue (see page 165)
1/4 teaspoon salt	
2 tablespoons cornstarch	

Preheat the oven to 450°. Prepare a single-crust, 9-inch pie shell, using the Flaky Paste recipe. Prick the bottom several times with a fork, and bake until lightly browned, 10 to 12 minutes.

In the top of a double boiler, combine the cottage cheese and half-and-half. Mix well. Sift together the sugar, salt, cornstarch, and add to the cottage cheese a little at a time. Cook over hot water while stirring until the mixture begins to thicken. In a small container, beat the egg yolks until creamy, and slowly add to the yolks several spoonfuls of the hot mixture, stirring constantly to avoid lumps. Then gradually add the yolks back to the hot mixture. Cook until it thickens to coat a spoon.

Blend in the lemon juice and rind, cook 2 or 3 minutes more, and pour the filling into the baked crust. Spoon the meringue on the custard. Lower the oven temperature to 325°, and bake until peaks are golden brown, about 10 to 15 minutes. *Makes 6 to 8 servings.*

⤲ AUNT GUSSIE'S FIG PIE ⤲

*A*unt Gussie's wealth was in her cooking expertise, which she began accumulating at age six. Her handwritten will bequeathed her secret recipes to her children, favorite nieces, and grandnieces. She left this one to my mama, who passed it on to me.

FIREPLACE RECIPE:

Pick a pint of ripe sweet figs, stem and wash good. Quarter them in bottom of usual raw pastry, and over same sprinkle grated rind of a lemon. To this put a mix of 2 eggs frothed, a half-pint freshly dripped clabber cheese which mash cow-pea size, a short half-pint of milk mostly cream, same of sugar, a little flour, pinch or two of salt, and pour the whole over figs. Bake in Dutch oven till pie sets and pastry is of a golden brown. If the heat once relaxes, the goodness of the pie is sure to be affected.

Best eaten when cold. Excellent served with thick layer of fresh-skimmed sweet cream.

MODERN METHOD:

$^1/_2$ recipe Flaky Paste (see page 157)	2 teaspoons lemon rind, grated
$^3/_4$ cup sugar	1 cup large curd cottage cheese, well drained
$^1/_2$ teaspoon salt	
1 tablespoon flour	2 cups ripe figs, washed and stemmed (if canned, drain well)
1 teaspoon cornstarch	
2 eggs, well beaten	Whipped cream or ice cream for topping
1 cup cream or half-and-half	

Prepare an unbaked, single-crust, 9-inch pastry shell, using the Flaky Paste recipe.

Preheat the oven to 350°. In a bowl, mix the sugar and salt with the flour and cornstarch. In a smaller container, blend the beaten eggs with the cream and lemon rind, and gradually stir them into the flour mix. Fold in the cottage cheese and pour the mix over the figs. Pour this into the unbaked pastry shell.

Bake 50 to 60 minutes in the oven or until the crust is light brown and a knife inserted near the center comes out clean. Chill before serving. Top with whipped cream or ice cream. *Makes 6 to 8 servings.*

⧉ APPLE "MERANGE" ⧉

*A*unt Lillie Mae's daughter had a hard time controlling her big appetite. When her weight got up to 325 pounds, she began collecting recipes for less fattening foods like this low-calorie apple pie. She loved this dish so much, she couldn't stop eating with fewer than three helpings.

FIREPLACE RECIPE:

First, take a deep dish and put a bottom crust into it, as for a pie; have nice sour apples, pared, sliced and stewed, sweetened slightly. Place a layer of the stewed apple upon the crust thicker than the usual, then put on a thin layer of sliced penny loaf-bread, spread with butter as for eating. Another layer of same. Place in the Dutch oven. Bake.

When done, have whites of eggs beaten, mixed with a little loaf sugar, say 3 eggs for a 2-quart dish; place this on merange and return to oven to brown the frosting. Serve with nutmeg spreading sauce.

MODERN METHOD:

1 recipe Flaky Paste (see page 157)	8 slices baker's bread
1/2 cup sugar	2 tablespoons margarine
2 cups stewed apples, slightly juicy, mashed coarsely, about 6 apples	Meringue (see page 165)

Make pastry as for a double-crust pie, using the Flaky Paste recipe. Roll out all the dough, and fit it into the bottom and up the sides of a 2-quart casserole.

Preheat the oven to 375°. In a saucepan, add the sugar to the apples, mix thoroughly, and place half the apples on the pastry in the casserole. Cut the crust from the bread. Spread the margarine sparingly on the bread, and lay the slices margarine-side-up on top of the apples in the casserole. Add another layer of apples and another layer of bread.

Bake in the oven about 15 to 18 minutes or until the top is golden brown. Remove and add the meringue while hot. Lower the heat to 325°, and bake 10 to 15 minutes until the peaks of the meringue are golden brown. Good with Nutmeg Spreading Sauce (see page 112). *Makes 8 to 10 servings.*

MOONSHINE CUSTARD

(previously called Whiskey or Mountain Dew Custard)

*O*n a very cold day in the dead of winter when this custard would hold its shape without extra effort, Cousin Evie made this recipe and took it to the sewing circle at the church. During refreshments, the ladies made so much noise, the preacher came from the parsonage to see what was going on. That's when Cousin Evie was thrown off Christ's bandwagon.

FIREPLACE RECIPE:

Take 6 eggs, the whites of, beat them in a broad plate to make a very stiff froth, then add gradually 6 tablespoons powdered sugar. Beat in 1 heaping tablespoon of favorite preserves, mushed. Put out to thoroughly chill.

In serving, pour into each saucer 2 or 3 big spoonfuls, sweetened and flavored as to liking, and on this, place a liberal portion of moonshine.

This quantity is enough for 6 hefty servings.

MODERN METHOD:

6   egg whites
6   tablespoons confectioners' sugar
1   heaping tablespoon fruit preserves
    Moonshine or alcoholic beverage that blends with preserves
    Whipped cream as desired.

Beat the egg whites until very stiff. Add the sugar gradually. Mash the preserves smooth with a fork, and blend them in. Chill thoroughly. Place 3 to 4 tablespoonfuls in a saucer or individual serving dish. Onto this, pour the moonshine or favorite liquor in the amount desired. Top each serving with the whipped cream. *Makes 6 servings.*

❧ COFFEE CUSTARD ❧

*A*fter being jilted, Grandma's daughter Gracie endeavored to protect her younger sister from men with her pranks. Promising "the way to win a man's heart is through his stomach," she obliged her sister by making this recipe for her to serve to her beau—but substituted salt for the sugar. He rushed away, bending over with a bad coughing spell.

FIREPLACE RECIPE:

Take 4 eggs, beat up to same color, add a half-pint of rich fresh milk and a cup of cold strong coffee. Put in sugar to taste mixed with a dash of flour, and cook in patty pan over finger of water in Dutch oven. A little lump of fresh-churned butter is fine.

MODERN METHOD:

³/₄ cup sugar, or to taste	4 eggs, well beaten
2 teaspoons cornstarch	1 teaspoon butter or margarine
³/₄ cup whole milk	1 cup whipped cream (optional)
1 cup strong coffee	

Mix the sugar and cornstarch in the top of a double boiler. Gradually blend in the milk and coffee. Cook over hot water 4 to 5 minutes, stirring steadily. Place the eggs in a small container, and slowly spoon in one-fourth of the hot mixture, stirring constantly. Then stir the egg mixture back into the double boiler. Continue cooking and stirring until the mixture lightly coats a spoon. Add the butter and remove from the heat. Pour into individual molds, chill, and serve cold. Top with sweetened whipped cream if desired. *Makes 6 servings.*

↩ ROCK CUSTARD ↪

*W*hile Grandpa thought Grandma burned lumps on the bottom of the custard pan, the kids yelled for more rocks.

FIREPLACE RECIPE:

Take a pint of rich milk and in it cook three handfuls of rice till very soft. Add a little sugar and a dash of salt. Steam a minute. When cool, add lumps of well congealed favorite jelly.

MODERN METHOD:

1   cup raw rice
2   cups whole milk
2   tablespoons sugar
$^1/_2$ teaspoon salt

$^1/_2$ cup ($^1/_4$-inch-cubed) congealed
       jelly, more if desired
       Whipped cream

Cook the rice in the milk until soft. Blend in the sugar and salt. Cook one more minute and remove from the heat. When the rice mixture is cool, add the jelly cubes, distributing them evenly. Top with whipped cream. *Makes 6 servings.*

THE COMMON GARDEN ROSE

This, the queen of flowers, is one of the most elegant and fragrant of vegetable productions. Its petals yield, on distillation, a small portion of aromatic oil, together with a *water* which possesses both the odour and the taste of flowers.

From the petals of this rose are also prepared a *conserve* and *syrup* which are used in medicine.

—From *Useful Knowledge* by Reverend William Bingley (1818)

CHEROKEE MAHALIA'S INDIAN PUDDING

This old Indian recipe has been a regular in our family for generations. Grandma often made trips to the nearby Cherokee village to visit the Chief's squaw, her fourth cousin, who taught her invaluable herbal cures. Among other things Grandma learned was the recipe for this scrumptious pudding.

FIREPLACE RECIPE:

Set Dutch oven having a little water on a trivet over hot coals. In patty-pan, mix 3 tea-cups of good fresh sweet milk heavy with cream and a half tea-cup of cornmeal and set in oven. Open. Stir till thickens, take out, and to it put a half-pint of good cane syrup, a walnut-size lump of butter, a little spoon of salt, and several pinches of ginger root ground fine and mix well.

Set pan back in oven, cover, and cook over slow coals till begins to set, then pour over it a half-pint of same good rich milk, give it a stir, cover, and bake over very slow coals 2 to 3 hours. Serve at once with layer of thick sweet cream.

MODERN METHOD:

$^1/_2$ cup cornmeal	1 teaspoon salt
3 plus 1 cups whole milk	3 tablespoons butter or margarine, melted
1 cup dark molasses	$^1/_2$ teaspoon ginger

Preheat the oven to 300°. Place the cornmeal in the top of a double boiler. Add 3 cups milk and mix thoroughly. Set over boiling water and stir until the mixture slightly coats a spoon. Add the molasses, salt, butter, and ginger.

Pour the mixture into a buttered 2-quart casserole, and bake in the oven 20 minutes. At this time, pour the remaining 1 cup milk over the pudding; give a few stirs, but don't thoroughly mix. Bake 2 more hours until brown, and until the pudding quivers only in the center when shaken. Serve warm with half-and-half or ice cream. *Makes 8 servings*.

HOLIDAY YAM PUDDING

I loved trips with Grandma to the country store. She always gave me a penny to buy a piece of candy from one of the round glass jars lining the counter beside the cash register with the big swinging handle. I almost always chose a Tootsie Roll. Its taste reminded me of her wonderful yam pudding.

FIREPLACE RECIPE:

Put 1 lb. small yams in sun a fortnight to render sweeter. Wash yams and boil in covering of water over simmering coals till tender. Peel and run through tammis* to mush. Into this add 1 tea-cup fine white sugar and a half as much fresh-churned butter which has been well mixed. Then add a half-dozen well-beaten yolks of fresh-laid eggs, the rasped rind of a small lemon but not an atom of white, one tea-cup of orange juice, and a dash of salt. Beat each well after adding. Fold in the egg whites beaten to stiff, and gently mix the whole thoroughly together.

Pour mix into a well-buttered patty-pan, sprinkle top with fine white sugar. Set patty-pan in hot Dutch oven containing a little bottom water. Cover. Put a few coals in lid and bake over slack coals till done. Serve with thick sweet cream. Makes for family of 10.

MODERN METHOD:

$2^1/_2$ cups cooked, mashed yams, about 1 pound

$1^1/_4$ cups sugar, plus 2 tablespoons for sprinkling

$^1/_2$ teaspoon salt

$^1/_2$ cup butter or margarine, melted

6 eggs, separated, save whites

$1^1/_2$ teaspoons grated lemon rind

1 cup orange juice

Whipped cream, for serving

Preheat the oven to 350°. Peel the yams, cut them into cubes, and boil them until tender. Mash until creamy. Mix together the $1^1/_4$ cups sugar, salt, and butter, and add to the yams. Beat the egg yolks, and add them to the yams along with the grated lemon rind and orange juice, beating well after each addition. Whip the egg whites to a stiff froth and fold into the mixture.

Pour the pudding into a greased 2-quart casserole, and sprinkle the top with the remaining 2 tablespoons sugar. Bake in the oven 30 to 40 minutes until firm. Serve with whipped cream. *Makes 8 large servings.*

*A colander.

COUSIN LUDIE MAE'S BREAD PUDDING WITH LEMON SYRUP

(alias Angel Pie)

*C*ousin Ludie Mae would not try this recipe because it contained leftover bread—and scraps were for the hogs. When relatives served it to her as "Angel Pie," her praises never ended.

FIREPLACE RECIPE:

Put scraps of biscuit bread in a round baking pan. In a stew pan, put 1½ pints fresh sweet milk, mix in half-pint sugar. Put 3 fresh eggs beaten to same color, dash of salt, of nutmeg. Pour over bread. Put pan in Dutch oven with water. Bake over slack coals. Put on lemon syrup.

Now the syrup. Place in pan a scant half-pint sugar, same of milk, a bit of flour, dash of salt, and boil over water till slightly thickened. Take up and add juice of a big lemon, a little rind, dollop of butter, and it is ready.

MODERN METHOD:

Bread Pudding

1	cup sugar	3	cups milk
3	eggs, beaten	4½	cups bread cubes
¼	teaspoon salt		Lemon Syrup (recipe follows)
⅛	teaspoon nutmeg		or other topping

Preheat the oven to 350°. Combine the sugar, eggs, salt, and nutmeg in the top of a double boiler and gradually blend in the milk. Cook over hot water, stirring constantly until the mixture heavily coats a spoon. Remove from the heat. Add the bread cubes and mix lightly.

Pour the mixture into a baking dish, and place it in a large shallow pan on the center rack of the oven. Pour hot water into a larger pan to the depth of 1 inch. Bake in the oven about 10 to 15 minutes, or until a tester inserted in the center comes out clean. Serve with Lemon Syrup or other topping. *Makes 6 servings.*

Lemon Syrup

1 cup sugar	$^1/_3$ cup lemon juice
2 tablespoons cornstarch	$^1/_2$ teaspoon grated lemon rind
$^1/_8$ teaspoon salt	2 tablespoons butter or margarine
$^3/_4$ cup milk	

Mix the sugar, cornstarch, and salt in the top of a double boiler. Gradually blend in the milk. Cook over boiling water, stirring, until slightly thick. Add the lemon juice, rind, and butter. Cook 1 more minute. Remove from the heat. The mixture will be thin. *Makes about 1 cup.*

CURE OF RHEUMATISM

Take cucumbers, when full grown, and put them into a pot with a little salt; then put the pot over a slow fire, where it should remain for about an hour. Take the cucumbers and press them, the juice from which must be put into bottles, corked up tight, and placed in the cellar, where they should remain for about a week; then wet a flannel rag with the liquid, and apply it to the parts affected.

—From *Mackenzie's Five Thousand Receipts* (1852)

⌒ POUND PUDDING ⌒

*A*unt Lettie Mae, Grandma's oldest sister, smoked a corn-cob pipe. She declared eating this cake took the tobacco stain off her teeth.

FIREPLACE RECIPE:

Take of raisins well stoned, but not chopped, and currants well washed, 1 lb. each. Add ¼ lb. of flour or bread very finely crumbled, 3 ozs. sugar, 1½ ozs. grated lemon peel, ½ of a small nutmeg grated, ½ dozen of eggs, well beaten. Work well together, put in a cloth, tie firmly, allowing room to swell. Put into boiling water in saucepan on trivet and boil not less than two hours. Keep boiling for this time.

The cloth, when about to be used, should be dipped into boiling water, squeezed dry, and floured; when the pudding is done, have a pan of cold water ready, dip it in for a moment soon as it comes from pot to prevent the pudding from sticking to the cloth.

MODERN METHOD:

1 cup seedless raisins, coarsely chopped	½ teaspoon nutmeg
1 cup currants	3 tablespoons sugar
1 tablespoon lemon rind, grated	3 eggs, well beaten
½ cup all-purpose flour	

Combine the raisins, currants, and grated lemon rind. Sift the flour, nutmeg, and sugar and add to the raisin mixture. Blend in the eggs.

Dip a muslin cloth in boiling water, squeeze it dry, and flour it. Place the mixture in the muslin cloth, and tie it firmly, allowing room to swell. Place the cloth in boiling water and boil at least 2 hours. When done, remove the cloth from the boiling water and dip it in cold water for a moment. This prevents the pudding from sticking to the cloth. Untie the cloth and pour the pudding into a serving dish. Serve warm or cold. Good with Nutmeg Spreading Sauce (see page 112). *Makes 6 servings.*

NOTE: The pudding can be baked in a casserole at 350° for 25 to 30 minutes, but it does not have the same delicate flavor. Test for doneness with a toothpick.

↞ KISS PUDDING ↠

$\mathcal{C}$ousin Viola made this often to give her bachelor son a nudge.

FIREPLACE RECIPE:

Boil quart fresh sweet milk in custard kettle, stir into it 4 piling up tablespoons sugar and proper thickening flour dissolved in a little milk and added to well beaten and strained yolks of 4 eggs.

Turn into greased pan, sides sprinkled with a little loose sugar. Beat whites of eggs stiff, add cup or so of pulverized sugar, dash of vanilla, spread on top of pudding. When done, spread with grated coconut.

MODERN METHOD:

2 cups milk	2 egg whites, stiffly beaten
2^1/$_2$ tablespoons sugar	^{1}/$_2$ cup confectioners' sugar
2 tablespoons cornstarch	^{1}/$_2$ teaspoon vanilla extract
2 tablespoons milk for dissolving cornstarch	^{1}/$_2$ cup sweetened flaked coconut
2 egg yolks, well beaten	

Preheat the oven to 400°. In a double boiler, place the milk, sugar, cornstarch dissolved in the 2 tablespoons milk, and egg yolks. Cook over hot water until slightly thick, stirring constantly. Pour in a 2-quart casserole.

Beat the egg whites to a stiff froth, adding the powered sugar gradually. Blend in the vanilla and spread the mixture on top of the pudding. Quickly set the casserole in the oven. Remove as soon as the egg whites begin to brown. Spread with the coconut flakes. Serve cold. *Makes 8 servings.*

∽ J.B.'S PEAR HONEY PUDDIN'-PIE ∽

*A*unt Cassie had to make this dessert for Uncle J.B. at least once a month. He said it cranked up a good disposition. Called it his "getting-along" pie.

FIREPLACE RECIPE:

Three layer Pie. Use a jar of pear honey from pantry or take a half-dozen sand pears, peel and core and grind coarse. Cook in pot with equal amount of sugar to honey-stage and add a little marmalade, orange or lemon, as desired.

Make tea cakes: To a half-pint sugar put hickory nut-size lump of butter, rub together, and put two fresh-laid eggs, a hefty quarter pint sweet cream; beat smooth. Put seasoned flour and knead till greatly stiff. Roll thin and cut into cakes with small glass top. Cook in quick oven.

Cook pudding in pan over water in Dutch oven. Put together 3 cups good fresh sweet milk, half-pint sugar, proper thickening, pinch of salt, vanilla beans, cook till hot, then mix in 2 beaten eggs, and cook same till thickens. Remove beans. Add a little butter and do while hot. In serving dish, make layers of tea cakes, pear honey. Pudding between each, having pudding on top. Sprinkle with tea cake crumbs.

MODERN METHOD:

Pear Honey

5	cups Bosc or granular pears, peeled and cored, finely ground
4	cups sugar (less if pears are very sweet)
$^1/_2$	cup favorite marmalade or canned crushed pineapple, drained

In a saucepan, mix the pears, sugar, and marmalade. Simmer over low heat, stirring often until the pears are tender and the juice is thick as honey. The cooking time varies depending on the pears. When done, there should be very little juice. *Makes 4 cups.*

Tea Cakes

$^1/_3$	cup sugar	1	teaspoon vanilla extract
$^1/_4$	cup butter or margarine, melted	$1^1/_2$	teaspoons baking powder
1	egg, beaten	$^3/_4$	teaspoon salt
$^1/_3$	cup half-and-half	2	cups all-purpose flour plus flour for kneading

Preheat the oven to 375°. Combine the sugar, melted butter, egg, half-and-half, and vanilla in a bowl and mix well. Sift the baking powder and salt with the flour, and add gradually to the mixture, stirring after each addition.

Knead the dough until stiff, and roll to ¼-inch thickness on a lightly floured board. Cut the dough into cakes with a biscuit cutter, and bake for 20 to 25 minutes or until golden but not brown; the cakes burn easily. *Makes about 18 tea cakes.*

Pudding and Assembly

1	cup sugar	3	cups milk
4	tablespoons cornstarch	2	eggs
2	tablespoons flour	1	tablespoon butter or margarine
¼	teaspoon salt	2	teaspoons vanilla extract

In the top of a double boiler, mix together the sugar, cornstarch, flour, and salt. Blend in the milk. Cook until the mixture begins to coat the back of a spoon, stirring constantly.

In a small bowl, beat the eggs and dribble in several spoonfuls of hot liquid while stirring briskly. Return the mixture slowly to the double boiler, stirring constantly. Cook until the mixture coats the spoon well. Remove from the heat, add the butter and vanilla, and blend.

In a 2-quart or larger casserole, place a layer of one-third of the pear honey. Spread over this a layer of tea cakes, about 5, each broken into six or eight pieces. Over the cakes, spoon one-third of the custard. Save one tea cake for topping crumbs. Repeat until there are three layers of each, ending with custard. Sprinkle the top with fine tea cake crumbs. Cover and set aside at least 2 hours for ingredients to blend before serving. Best when cool. *Makes 8 servings.*

VARIATION: For *Banana Puddin'-Pie*, substitute 2 or 3 bananas sliced medium-thin for the pear honey. Add sugar to the custard, if desired.

GRANDMA'S CHEESECAKE PUDDING

*L*adies carried what they made best to the All-Day Singing and Dinner on the Ground at Grandma's church and often swapped recipes. This is one she never put up for swap.

FIREPLACE RECIPE:

Take 15 slices of 3-day-old bread from penny loaf and 5 stale biscuits. Cover with hot water, mash out water. Add powdered ginger, nutmeg, salt, a quick stream of rose water. Put ½ pint sugar, a handful currants. Put in a fresh-laid egg beaten till yolk and white are indistinguishable.

Place the whole in a well greased patty-pan, dot with a little butter, then place pan in Dutch oven over slow coals until set. Turn out.

Serve cold with thin coat of sweet cream, boiled vanilla sauce, or coffee sauce.

MODERN METHOD:

22 slices stale bread (about a loaf)	½ teaspoon vanilla and ½ teaspoon almond extract, mixed
1 cup sugar	
2 eggs, beaten	1 tablespoon butter
½ teaspoon grated nutmeg	½ pint whipped cream
1 teaspoon powdered ginger	Vanilla Sauce (optional, recipe follows)
¼ teaspoon salt	Coffee Sauce (optional, see page 106)
½ cup raisins	

Preheat the over to 325°. Pour hot water over the slices of bread in a bowl and leave until well soaked. Mash out the water. Add the sugar, beaten eggs, nutmeg, ginger, salt, raisins, and vanilla-almond extract and mix well.

Place the mixture in a well-greased casserole. Pack with a spoon. Lay bits of the butter on top. Bake for about 30 minutes, or until an inserted toothpick comes out clean. When cold, turn out of the casserole onto a serving dish. Serve cold, topped with a thin coat of whipped cream, Vanilla Sauce, or Coffee Sauce (see page 106). *Makes 8 servings.*

Vanilla Sauce

$^1/_2$ cup water	2 teaspoons vanilla extract
2 cups sugar	

Cook the water and sugar together until a little dropped in cold water forms a soft ball. Cool, add the vanilla, and beat until stiff enough to spread. *Makes $^3/_4$ cup.*

TIRES, TO KEEP ON THE WHEEL

A correspondent at the *Southern Planter* says: "I ironed a buggy for my own use seven years ago, and the tires are now as tight as when put on. My method of filling the fellies* with the (linseed) oil is as follows:

I use a long, cast iron oil heater, made for the purpose; the oil is brought to a boiling heat, the wheel is placed on a stick, so as to hang in the oil, each felly an hour, for the common sized felly.

The timber should be dry, as green timber will not take oil. Care should be taken that the oil not be made hotter than a boiling heat, in order that the timber not be burnt. Timber filled with oil is not susceptible to water, and is much more durable."

*Rims of a wheel supported by spokes.

—From *Dr. Chase's Recipes* (1867)

☙ SWEETIE PIE ❧

*G*randma said when she first tried out her amazing new 1915 wood stove with this pie, she sat rocking on the porch shedding happy tears.

FIREPLACE RECIPE:

For macaroni, make stiff dough, cut into strips hand-long and roll over big end of sage broomstraw let dry in sun. Remove broomstraw. Cut hardened dough into small pieces and boil in milk with lemon rind till tender. Remove rind and place in baking dish. Beat some eggs, add sugar, adequate milk, and pour over macaroni and bake.

MODERN METHOD:

1 cup (1-inch) pieces macaroni	3 eggs, well beaten
1 pint plus 1 pint milk	$^1/_2$ cup sugar
Rind of $^1/_2$ lemon	$^3/_4$ cup choice preserves

Preheat the oven to 325°. Simmer the macaroni in 1 pint milk with the lemon rind for 10 minutes until tender. Remove the rind, drain, and place the macaroni in a casserole.

In a separate bowl, mix the eggs and the remaining pint of milk with the sugar. Pour over the macaroni. Bake for 30 to 35 minutes. Test with a knife inserted at the edge. When cool, top with strawberry, blueberry, or other preserves. *Makes 8 servings.*

GENERAL RULES FOR PRESERVING LIFE AND HEALTH

"Keep the feet warm; the head cool; and the body open." If these were generally attended to, the physician's aid would seldom be required.

—From *Mackenzie's Five Thousand Receipts* (1852)

MAHALIA'S BUTTERMILK ICE CREAM

*T*he first bite of this goody brought a wince from the slightly sour tang—then the tongue took to it like a baby to a sugar tit.*

FIREPLACE RECIPE:

Take a half gallon or more buttermilk and add sugar to taste. Mix in a few vanilla beans. Let stand a little while then take out beans. Freeze.

MODERN METHOD:

3   quarts buttermilk, strained to remove lumps
2   cups sugar, or to taste
2   teaspoons vanilla extract

Mix the buttermilk, sugar, and vanilla together with an eggbeater until very smooth. Pour into a gallon ice cream freezer container, insert the paddles, cover, and set the container in the outer bucket. Fill the bucket with cracked ice, and turn the freezer handle until too hard to turn. The ice cream is then frozen. *Makes 3 quarts.*

*A little sugar tied in porous cloth to form a ball.

ICE CREAM

To prevent its chilling the stomach, dust it with a little pepper. The cream destroys the taste of the pepper.

—From *The Housekeeper Cook Book* (1894)

⋙ WINE SALAD ⋘

*G*randma said she got this jewel from her eight-party-line telephone grapevine. That was the day Elvira caught her listening to her private recipe and called her a thief.

Grandpa loved her new gelatin recipe after he doodled a hole in the center and filled the hole with his special sauce—wine. It tasted so good that the wine became a regular part of Grandma's recipe.

FIREPLACE RECIPE:

Grandma bought a package of unflavored gelatin at the Trading Post. At home she mixed it with hot water, cranberries, pineapple, and wine. After it congealed, she cut it into 2-inch cubes.

MODERN METHOD:

1   (^{1}/4-ounce) package unflavored gelatin (such as Knox)
1^3/4 cups boiling water
^{3}/4 cup favorite wine

^{1}/2 cup canned crushed pineapple, drained
1^1/2 cups cranberries, cooked and diced
4   tablespoons cream cheese
3   tablespoons sour cream

In a large bowl, blend together the gelatin, water, wine, pineapple, and cranberries. Pour into a mold or glass dish. Refrigerate until jelled. For the topping, mix together the cream cheese and sour cream. Spoon the topping on the salad in the bowl, or spoon it on individual servings. *Makes 6 medium servings.*

BURNS

Wet a soft cloth in strong soapsuds, sprinkle thickly with soda and bind on the affected part.

—From *The Housekeeper Cook Book* (1894)

Candy and Snacks

∽ PARTY POPCORN BALLS ∽

*P*opcorn balls held together with molasses were plentiful at church socials during syrup-making season. Dozens of gallon buckets of syrup were filled from the long, shallow metal cistern where sugarcane juice was cooked to molasses over a sprawling hot fire.

FIREPLACE RECIPE:

Pop 3 quarts popcorn in skillet on trivet over high heat, shaking and rocking pan constantly. Remove from fire, discard hard kernels. Let wait.

Mix a half-pint of molasses with three-fourths-pint of white sugar combined with a little brown, a little water, a bit of cider vinegar, and a few dashes of salt. Boil all to crack stage.

Put to this a little butter and pour syrup over popcorn. Mix together well and form small balls, closing hands on same until firm together. Lay separate.

MODERN METHOD:

3 quarts popped popcorn, free of hard kernels

1 cup molasses, preferably pure cane

1 cup granulated sugar

$^1/_2$ cup brown sugar, packed

$^1/_4$ cup water

$^1/_4$ cup cider vinegar

$^1/_2$ teaspoon salt

1 tablespoon butter or margarine

Pop $3^1/_2$ ounces popcorn in popper, or use 1 package microwave light popcorn, and adjust the salt and butter above. Place in a large mixing bowl.

In a saucepan, mix the molasses, sugars, water, vinegar, and salt, and boil until a bit of syrup dropped into cold water separates into threads that are hard but not brittle. Add the butter to the syrup, mix well, and dribble on the popcorn, stirring until all is well mixed.

Press tightly into 2-inch-in-diameter balls (or smaller or larger to suit). Place on waxed paper and serve when cool. *Makes 6 to 8 servings, depending on the size of balls.*

NOTE: Besides being party fare, this is also a delightful rainy-day project for youngsters.

ANGEL FOOD POPCORN

*T*he first time Aunt Hattie made a batch of syrup for this popcorn, she discovered it was cooked too long. She poured it in the dogs' feeding pan to give them a treat. Next morning she had to soak their snouts with wet rags before they could open their mouths.

FIREPLACE RECIPE:

Pop popcorn to give 3 quarts in a greased skillet on trivet over high heat. Rock pan to turn kernels constantly. Remove from fire, discard hard kernels, and sprinkle on a little salt. Into this, mix 4 handfuls of pecans cut fine.

Mix well together in suitable pot a half-pint of the finest sugar, same of molasses, a few vanilla beans, and set on trivet over medium coals on hearth. Stir while cooking. When a drop becomes hard in cold water, take from heat in haste. Best to test often. Discard beans, put in butter and stir, and quickly pour over popcorn. Mix all well together; rush same to a long narrow earthen pan of well-buttered bottom and sides, and press firm down. Strew pecans finely grated on top.

Slice when cold.

MODERN METHOD:

3	quarts popped popcorn	$^1/_2$	teaspoon salt
1	teaspoon butter or margarine	1	cup molasses
2	cups pecans, chopped	$1^1/_2$	teaspoons vanilla
1	cup sugar	$^1/_2$	cup pecans, grated in blender, for top

Grease a 9 x 13 x 2-inch pan. Pop $3^1/_2$ ounces popcorn in a popper, or for microwave, use 1 package light popcorn. Place the popcorn in a large bowl, and mix in the butter and pecans.

To make the syrup, place the sugar, salt, and molasses in a saucepan, and stir constantly over medium heat until a drop forms a hard ball in cold water. Remove from the heat immediately, before it cooks to an unwanted cracking stage. Stir in the vanilla. Quickly pour the syrup over the popcorn and mix to cover each grain.

Pour in a buttered dish and pack firmly. Top with grated pecans and press to adhere. When cold, slice and serve. *Makes 8 servings.*

⌒ PARCHED (TOASTED) PECANS ⌒

*A*fter Aunt Lillie Mae got this pecan recipe from her grandmother, she kept a fruit jar full in her cupboard. When it got pretty well down, she made another batch because she said you couldn't get satisfaction out of less than a few handfuls.

FIREPLACE RECIPE:

Melt some butter in open spider and to this put a batch of shelled pecan halves. Stir butter and a little salt on all.

Roast over slow coals, stirring constantly as with parching coffee until they are a nice brown. Upon taking up, sprinkle with a little salt.

MODERN METHOD:

4 cups shelled pecan halves
$1/2$ cup (1 stick) butter or margarine, melted
$1/2$ teaspoon salt, or to taste

Preheat the oven to 250°. Coat the pecans with the melted butter, sprinkle with the salt, and spread in one layer in a baking pan. Bake in the oven 55 to 65 minutes or until lightly browned, stirring often. When cool, store in an airtight container. Good snack or party fare. *Makes 4 cups.*

MOTHS

Remove from the room or closet everything that burning camphor will injure. Leave all woolens, etc., hanging. Put a small piece of camphor into an iron dish on an iron or earthen stand; set it on fire; it burns quickly and nothing should be near it. Leave the doors closed for an hour, open them wide; remove everything and hang to air thoroughly.

—From *The Housekeeper Cook Book* (1894)

NYAWH LEENS PECAN PRAWLEENS

(translated: New Orleans Pecan Pralines)

*U*ncle Nate, Aunt Caroline's husband, worked for the Southern Railroad Company, and it transferred him to New Orleans. Caroline sent Grandma many new recipes. Among them was this one. Besides passing it around to all the relatives, she made a batch every Christmas as a special treat.

FIREPLACE RECIPE:

Mix some white and brown sugar, add a little milk and sweet cream and some maple or cane syrup, and 2 vanilla beans. Cook till slightly thick, add a double handful of pecan halves, and mix in a little butter. Drop by spoonfuls on platter, a pecan half in each spoon.

MODERN METHOD:

$^1/_4$ cup milk	1 cup maple syrup
$^1/_4$ cup cream	3 cups pecan halves, more if desired
1 cup granulated sugar	1 teaspoon butter or margarine
$^1/_2$ cup brown sugar	$^1/_4$ teaspoon vanilla extract

Combine the milk and cream in a saucepan. Add the sugars and syrup and mix well. Boil, stirring constantly, until the mixture forms a soft ball in cold water. Add the pecans. Boil 2 or 3 more minutes or until the syrup makes a firm ball in cold water. Watch carefully and do not overcook. Remove from the heat and blend in the butter and vanilla.

Drop the mixture with the tip of a spoon onto a butter-greased platter about 5 inches apart, one pecan half in each patty. When cold, wrap individually. *Makes 30 to 40 pralines.*

COUSIN LULU'S NUTTY FIG BARS

*C*ousin Lulu was often called the nutty cousin because she never made any confection without nuts.

FIREPLACE RECIPE:

Make pastry for 2-crust pie, roll out, and cut in squares. On each square, put some figs, chopped pecans, and a little sugar and bake.

MODERN METHOD:

1	recipe Flaky Paste (see page 157)	$^1/_2$	cup ground pecan meats
1	beaten egg	$^1/_2$	cup granulated sugar
2	cups ripe figs	$^1/_4$	cup confectioners' sugar

Make the pastry as for a double-crust pie, using the Flaky Paste recipe. Roll half the dough $^3/_8$ inch thick in the shape of a square. Place on a baking sheet and spread the bottom lightly with half of the beaten egg.

Preheat the oven to 325°. Wash, stem, and chop the figs. Place them evenly on the pastry, and sprinkle them with the pecan meats. Mix the sugars and spread them on top of the pecans.

Roll out the other half of the dough to the size of the bottom piece, and place it over the fig mix. Press the dough together at the sides. Spread with the remaining beaten egg. Bake in the oven 20 to 25 minutes or until the top is a nice brown. Remove from the oven. Cut into squares with a sharp knife. *Makes 9 bars.*

CHRONIC RHEUMATISM

Has been cured by taking the bark of a bearing crab-apple tree, and putting a sufficient amount of it into whisky to make it *very* strong, then taking a wine-glass three times daily, until a gallon was used.

—From *Dr. Chase's Recipes* (1867)

~ STRAWBERRY COCONUTS ~

*T*he ladies of Grandma's social club lived within a five-mile circle. Periodically they met at the different homes with their Sears Roebuck catalogs to discuss the latest fashions. When the group met at her house during strawberry season, she served these coconuts.

FIREPLACE RECIPE:

Take a pint of big, ripe strawberries, wash and trim and dry them well. Cover with a smooth batter of egg, creamy milk, flour, baking powder, sugar, a pinch of salt, and a little vanilla.

In spider pan or deep skillet set over hot coals, quickly fry a few at a time in deep lard until brown. Cool berries, then dip in thick cream and roll in sweet coconut flakes. Lay out separate.

MODERN METHOD:

2 cups large, fresh, ripe strawberries

$^1/_4$ cup milk

$^1/_4$ cup cream or half-and-half

1 egg, beaten

1 cup all-purpose flour

$^3/_4$ teaspoon baking powder

1 tablespoon sugar

$^1/_4$ teaspoon salt

$^1/_4$ teaspoon vanilla

Oil for frying

$^1/_2$ cup sour cream diluted with 1 tablespoon water

$^1/_2$ cup shredded, sweetened coconut

Wash and trim the strawberries. Mix the milk and cream. Make a smooth batter of the egg, milk, flour, baking powder, sugar, salt, and vanilla.

Take 2 or 3 strawberries at a time, dip in the batter to thoroughly coat, and deep-fry in very hot oil 1 to $1^1/_2$ minutes or until very light brown. Do not overcook. Carefully remove the strawberries and drain on a paper towel. Continue until all are browned, taking care not to let the oil burn.

When cool, dip the browned strawberries one by one into the sour cream, and then roll each in the coconut. Lay them spaced apart on a tray. Refrigerate. Serve cold. *Makes 8 to 10 servings.*

❦ MOLASSES PULL CANDY ❦

*G*randma said in her young days when she was trying to capture Grandpa, she cooked this candy and invited him to meet her at the church for a candy-pulling to-do. As she was placing her pot of warm candy on the table beside the others, she looked up and saw him, released one hand from the pot, and waved.

He cleaned molasses off her shoes and the floor while embarrassment blurred her vision.

FIREPLACE RECIPE:

Put together molasses and half as much sugar and a little vinegar in a boiler and cook on hearth coals till forms a firm ball in cold water. Stir in a dollop of fresh-churned butter, mix and pour up. When cool, pull till hard.

Twist and lay on greased plate. Cut or break in pieces when cold.

MODERN METHOD:

1	cup sugar	$1/4$ teaspoon soda
1	tablespoon cider vinegar	2 tablespoons butter or margarine
2	cups sugarcane molasses	

Combine the sugar and vinegar in a 2-quart stainless steel saucepan. Blend in the molasses and cook uncovered over slow heat until the mix forms a firm ball in cold water. Remove from the heat. Add the soda and butter, mix well, and pour onto a greased platter.

When cool enough to handle, butter-grease your hands and pull and fold the mixture until hard. It is customary for two persons to pull together. The candy will become lighter in color. Twist it barber-pole-style and place on a buttered plate. When cold, break or cut into pieces. *Makes enough for about 3 couples.*

⚬⚬ ORANGE MARSHMALLOWS ⚬⚬

*A*s Grandma told it, before she married Grandpa Ned, they went on an outing in the horse-drawn surrey with her friend Dulcie and her beau, B.J. First time either couple had been sparking unchaperoned. The girls made a lunch from their finest recipes, hoping to win the boys' hearts through their stomachs.

During the picnic under a grove of magnolias, Ned and B.J. couldn't seem to get enough of Grandma's marshmallows. Dulcie's big slabs of meringue-topped vinegar pie sat untouched while her dreams of winning B.J. vanished, that is, until B.J. dived into her pie. (See the recipe for Hattie's Vinegar Cake-Pie on page 164.)

FIREPLACE RECIPE:

Dissolve a quarter pound of gum arabic in ¾ pint of water by heating over a slow fire while stirring. When dissolved, strain it and add ¼ cup strained orange juice and a quarter pound powdered sugar and put pot in Dutch oven containing water over coals a little hot.

Cook and stir to a thick paste. Slowly add the well-beaten whites of 2 eggs. Pour into a pan slightly dusted with starch, and when cool, divide into squares. Roll in fine sugar and place in airtight container.

MODERN METHOD:

1 pound gum arabic	5 tablespoons cornstarch
¾ cup water	½ teaspoon vanilla
¼ cup orange juice, strained	2 egg whites, stiffly beaten
1 cup less 1 tablespoon confectioners' sugar plus extra for dusting	

Mix the gum arabic in the water in the top of a double boiler. Place over boiling water and stir constantly until the arabic is dissolved. Remove from the heat, strain, and add the orange juice and the sugar mixed with the cornstarch. Again place over boiling water. Cook, stirring, until the mixture becomes a thick paste that is not sticky. Remove from the heat. Add the vanilla and gradually fold in the egg whites.

Pour the mixture into a small square pan with sides, and freely dust the top with confectioners' sugar. When cool, cut into 1-inch squares. Roll to cover all sides in the sugar, and place on a rack spaced apart. If saving for future use, pack in airtight boxes. *Makes about 20 marshmallows*.

WATERMELON RIND CANDY

*T*he community held a house-raising for Grandma and Grandpa when they built their home. Folks for miles around came to help. Womenfolk brought all kinds of food, including Watermelon Rind Candy, which took Grandma's fancy. Afterwards, she kept a Mason jar full in the cupboard for company snacks.

FIREPLACE RECIPE:

Cut off green peeling from watermelon rind, leaving only white, and cut this into finger-size strips for a quart. Put in fast boiling water over hot fire a few minutes then drain. When cool, cover with water containing salt, a few spoons to a quart. Put aside as thus six hours, then drain and rinse rind and cook in new water until tender, then drain.

In saucepan cook appropriate sugar and water for syrup until a thread forms when dropped from a clean spoon. Put rind to syrup and cook slow until rind is clear and syrup forms a long thin thread. Remove rind. Drop each piece into refined sugar to coat, lay out to cool and dry.

A little lemon or orange peel added to syrup while cooking adds.

MODERN METHOD:

4 cups white part of watermelon rind, cut in strips as for french fries (rind on very small melons is too thin)	1 quart plus 1$\frac{1}{4}$ cups water $\frac{1}{4}$ cup salt 2 cups sugar plus for coating Peel of average-size lemon, sliced

Cover the rind with hot water and boil 5 minutes. Drain. When cool, cover with a brine of 1 quart water and $\frac{1}{4}$ cup salt. Set aside at least 6 hours. Drain and rinse several times, and then cover the rind with fresh water and simmer until tender. Drain.

In a saucepan, place 2 cups sugar, the remaining 1$\frac{1}{4}$ cups water, and the lemon peel. Cook until a drop forms a soft ball in cold water. Add the rind. Simmer, stirring and lifting the rind from the bottom of the pan to prevent scorching. Cook until the rind is clear and the syrup forms a long thread. Remove the rind and drain. Discard the lemon peel if desired.

Drop each piece of rind in sugar for coating, shake off the excess, and lay the rinds separately on a rack to cool and dry. *Makes 8 to 10 servings.*

FRENCH-FRIED WATERMELON STICKS

The quilting bee at the church was a wonderful place to learn new recipes. Grandma always added her own touch, as with this snack.

FIREPLACE RECIPE:

Take rind from half a watermelon and cut off green peeling and any iota of pink. Slice rind into finger-long pencil-size sticks, and cover each with a batter of egg, salt, a few dashes of cinnamon, and equal amount of flour and cornmeal. Roll in flour and drop in deep hot lard in a spider pan, not to crowd. Sizzle a few minutes until light brown. Roll in fine white sugar and keep warm in heated Dutch oven until served.

MODERN METHOD:

$^1/_2$ cup all-purpose flour

$^1/_2$ cup cornmeal

$1^1/_4$ teaspoons salt

$^1/_2$ teaspoon cinnamon

1 egg, beaten

3 cups white watermelon rind cut into strips $^1/_4$-inch thick by 3 inches long

Flour for dredging

Shortening, melted 1-inch deep in frying pan

Sugar for coating

Mix the flour, cornmeal, salt, cinnamon, and egg into a batter. Coat the melon strips with the batter, and then roll in the flour. Fry in hot shortening 7 to 8 minutes, browning on all sides. Do not crowd. Remove the sticks from the pan and, while hot, roll in the sugar, coating heavily. Best served warm. *Makes 8 to 10 servings.*

⌒ SYRUP JUG ⌒

*I*n midafternoon a group of grandchildren swarmed Grandma's kitchen knowing something good was coming. The kids watched as Grandma held a warm biscuit sideways, made a hole with her finger two-thirds of the way down the biscuit, and filled the hole with syrup or molasses. They continually chanted, "More, more, Grandma. I'll hold it straight up and if it runs over, my tongue will catch it."

FIREPLACE RECIPE:

There was no written recipe for this easy treat.

MODERN METHOD:

The same basic recipe is used today.

HAIR—PREVENT FALLING OUT

To remedy hair splitting, the ends should be singed every 6 weeks to seal up the brittle hollow tubes, and if the hair is uneven, roll it in small twists, and singe these the entire length to catch all the ends. A solution of one handful of salt in a half a pint of rainwater will keep the hair from falling out.

—From *The Housekeeper Cook Book* (1894)

Cures and Potions

∽ LOVE POTION ∽

Grandma was fifteen when she fell in love with Grandpa, a carpetbagger's son. Sadly, besides his being across the social line, he was betrothed to a rich Yankee girl. With the will of a red-headed woodpecker on a dead oak, she went after him and won him with this Love Potion, a concoction from our Cherokee ancestors.

Although Grandma made sure this rub-on potion did not touch anyone's lips, we don't use it today because it is injurious to the body if a person drinks it.

FIREPLACE RECIPE:

Part 1 of 3 parts: In small patty pan, cut up two dozen male fronds from wild ferns. Add one cup of water and set pan in Dutch oven over slow coals, a few coals in lid. Simmer down to ½ cup of juice. Take from heat, drain through fine cloth, discard sediment. When cool, place juice back in pan, put in three hefty pinches of flour, stir constantly till well-thickened and creamy-smooth. Take from heat, destroy all but 1 tablespoonful.

Part 2 of 3 parts: Chop finely ¼ cup mayapple (mandrake) root, cover and steep in ¼ cup boiling water for 5 minutes, as for tea. Stir. Save ¼ teaspoon and destroy balance. This is **injurious to body if drank.**

Part 3 of 3 parts: Simmer 1 heaping teaspoon finely chopped elecampane rootstock in 1 cup water in patty-pan in Dutch oven on slow coals for one hour to render tincture. Add a little water if necessary, do not let cook dry. Strain. Destroy all but ¼ teaspoon. **Injurious to body if drank.**

To 1 tablespoon fern frond decoction (step 1) add ¼ teaspoon mayapple tea (step 2); mix, and add ¼ teaspoon elecampane tincture (step 3). Mix all well together.

While fresh, apply ¼ teaspoon of mixture to middle finger of right hand and swipe on left arm of intended. Destroy balance.

MODERN METHOD:

This potion is not used today because it injurious to the body if a person drinks it.

TICKLE DROPS

*G*randma claimed the minute her grandchildren saw a jar of Tickle Drops on the kitchen cabinet, they began a tune of hacking coughs that sounded like "Dixie."

FIREPLACE RECIPE:

Take a pint of double-refined sugar, sift it through a hair sieve, then a silk sieve. Put sugar and ½ pint molasses in small pan with a lip, add ½ pint boiling water and a little fresh-churned butter. Place on hot fire and have ready a buttered tin plate.

Take the pan of hot liquid in the right hand, and hold in the left a bit of iron, copper, or silver wire, 4 inches long to take off the drop from the lip of the pan, and let it run down and fall on the tin plate. When cold, mash drops with finger and take drops off plate with thin blade of a knife. Separate and wrap in thin oiled paper or they will all become one.

MODERN METHOD:

2	cups sugar	1	tablespoon butter
1	cup sugarcane molasses	¼	teaspoon oil of peppermint
1	cup boiling water		

Mix the sugar, molasses, boiling water, and butter in an uncovered saucepan, and cook on medium heat, stirring occasionally until the threads separate when dropped from a spoon, or until the syrup forms a hard, yet pliable ball in cold water. Remove from the heat, cool, and add the peppermint.

While fairly hot, let the individual drops slide from a small spoon onto a buttered cookie sheet to desired size while the saucepan containing the balance sits over very low heat.

When the drops are cool, mash them flat with your finger, wrap individually in waxed paper, and store in an airtight container. *Makes 2 dozen.*

MILK SOUP

*G*randpa admitted to playing sick quite often so Grandma would make this goody for him.

FIREPLACE RECIPE:

Boil 2 quarts milk with a little salt, dash of powdered cinnamon, and a little sugar in saucepan. In a patty-pan, place a few thin slices bakery bread, and cover this with a little of the milk and keep hot on trivet on cool coals. Do not let boil.

Put with the milk, yolks of half dozen eggs well beaten, and over medium hot coals, stir till thickens. Pour over bread in patty-pan and serve warm. Good nourishing dish. Put only a dab of sugar if ailing is with stomach.

MODERN METHOD:

The same basic recipe is used today.

CHARCOAL FOR SICK HEADACHE

If laid cold on a burn it will speedily cause the pain to abate. In an hour, if the burn is superficial, the flesh will seem nearly healed. It will sweeten tainted meats. It forms an excellent poultice for wounds and sores, a teaspoon in half a glass of water often relieves sick headache.

—From *The Housekeeper Cook Book* (1894)

∽ WATERMELON SOUP ∽

*O*ne time Uncle Jeremiah had a severe spell of feeling "feather-legged," a general bad feeling of weakness in the knees. He felt so bad for so long, he rode old Charlie in to see the doctor. Among other instructions, he was told to eat plenty of watermelon. Aunt Bessie came up with this soup. It soon became the staple for those feeling poorly. In season, she canned pulp in Mason jars for similar ailments during the winter.

FIREPLACE RECIPE:

Cut ripe watermelon hearts into small pieces and mash to a pulp till a quart. Mix a hefty $1/4$ pint of unprocessed flour with a little of the pulp, put in a speck of salt, stir until smooth, and place all in saucepan.

Simmer over low coals while stirring, until soup begins to thicken and take up. Drop in a pecan-size lump of butter and stir well.

MODERN METHOD:

4 cups ripe, sweet watermelon puréed	$1/8$ teaspoon salt
$1/2$ cup plus 1 teaspoon whole wheat flour	2 teaspoons butter or margarine

Use the heart of the watermelon. Remove the seeds, dice the melon, place in the blender, and purée. Mix enough purée with the flour to make a smooth paste, and add back to the bulk of the melon. Add the salt.

Place the mixture in a saucepan and simmer over very low heat, stirring constantly until it thickens slightly. Remove from the heat while thin. (The flour is for substance, not for thickening.) Add the butter, more or less as to taste. Serve hot or cool. Good with Skillet Peanut Tea Cake (see page 148). *Makes 4 servings*.

⊱ INDEX ⊰